BORN OF ANGELS AND DEMONS

Born of Angels and Demons

A Three-Continent Journey from Homelessness to Happiness

Cara Kuma Kinté

"Born of Angels and Demons"

Copyright© 2024 Cara Kuma Kinté. All Rights Reserved.

Unauthorized duplication or distribution of this publication in any form is strictly prohibited. No part of this publication may be reproduced, stored in a retrieval system, or transmitted in any form or by any means, electronic, mechanical, photocopying, recording, or otherwise, without prior written permission from the author.

Dedications

To my late grandmother, Sen:

Whose love, wisdom, and strength were the foundation of my life. Through your stories and your way of living, you taught me to hold on to hope, even in the most challenging times. Your presence still guides me, and I carry your memory with me every day.

To my uncle, Baboulek:

For giving me the gift of living a life of luxury, but more importantly, for teaching me the values of respect, discipline, hard work, and dedication. You showed me that true wealth lies in character and in the way we treat others.

To my late mother, Marthe:

Through your illness, I had the chance to know you more deeply and understand the struggles you faced. In Belgium, I found forgiveness, and that has brought me peace. I will always treasure the time we had together.

To late Mr. Bernard:

Who saved me from the streets when I was homeless, gave me a home, enrolled me back in school, and offered me hope when I had none. You gave me the chance to rebuild my life, and for that, I am eternally grateful.

And to Guy:

For supporting me from across the world when I was in Cameroon, for bringing me to Belgium, and for helping me reinstate my legal status. Your steadfast care and generosity during that time gave me the opportunity to start again and build a new future. I will never forget the impact you had on my life.

Acknowledgments

To my children:

Who have been my greatest source of strength and inspiration. Your love has carried me through every challenge, and I am forever grateful for the joy you bring into my life.

To my friends and family:

For standing by me, offering encouragement, and reminding me of the power of perseverance. Your belief in me has made all the difference.

To the organizations and individuals:

Who played pivotal roles throughout my journey, especially those who helped me during my experiences with domestic violence in Raleigh, North Carolina. Your support has been a lifeline, and your work is truly inspiring.

To the wonderful people:

Who I've met at the YMCA in the sauna who listened to my stories and motivated me to transform them into this book. Your belief in this project is why it exists today.

To Kevin:

Whose thoughtful suggestions and support along the way have been greatly appreciated, I am truly grateful.

Author's Note

Dear Reader,

Writing *Born of Angels and Demons* has been a profoundly personal journey. This book is more than just a story; it is a piece of my life. It captures the challenges I have faced, the lessons I have learned, and the moments that have shaped me.

As you read, you will experience the struggles and triumphs that made me who I am today. The child born in the first chapter is me, and my story is about *Born of Angels and Demons* and the strength we find when we face life's toughest challenges.

This book would not exist without the support of the incredible people in my life. My grandmother, whose wisdom and strength still guide me; my uncle, who raised me and taught me so much; my children, who inspire me every day; my family and friends, who have always been there for me; and my partner, who has not only been my rock but has also played a crucial role in editing this book and shaping it into what it is today. I am so grateful to each of you.

As you read these pages, I hope you find something that speaks to your journey. There is always hope, no matter where you start or how hard the road may seem.

Thank you for letting me share my story with you.

With all my heart,

Cara Kuma Kinté

Contents

Chapter 1: A New Dawn in Douala 1

    Reflection 14

Chapter 2: Seeds of Resilience 18

    Reflection 30

Chapter 3: The New Beginning in Ngaoundéré 31

    Reflection 36

Chapter 4: A Growing Family and New Beginnings 37

    Reflection 42

Chapter 5: Arrival in Ngok Mapubi - Changes and Challenges 44

    Reflection 49

Chapter 6: The Painful Revelation 50

    Reflection 55

Chapter 7: A New Beginning and Unforeseen Tensions 56

    Reflection 61

Chapter 8: Shadows of Change 62

    Reflection 65

Chapter 9: Unraveling Secrets 66

Chapter 10: Echoes in the Forest 70
    Reflection 78

Chapter 11: Unraveling Truths 79
    Reflection 83

Chapter 12: Beyond the Familiar 84
    Reflection 90

Chapter 13: Hours of Uncertainty 91
    Reflection 103

Chapter 14: Lost and Found: The Streets of Yaoundé 104
    Reflection 118

Chapter 15: Against the Current 119
    Reflection 127

Chapter 16: The Path Forward 128
    Reflection 134

Chapter 17: The Return 135
    Reflection 144

Chapter 18: The Storm's Arrival and Aftermath 147
    Reflection 155

Chapter 19: Navigating Change 156

Reflection 164

Chapter 20: The Weight of Inheritance 165

Reflection 171

Chapter 21: Veil of Returning Secrets 173

Reflection 182

Chapter 22: Unspoken Words. 184

Reflection 190

Chapter 23: Crossing Borders, Journey to Brussels 191

Reflection 194

Chapter 24: Arriving in Brussels and Discovering Belgium 195

Chapter 25: Final Journey in Belgium 203

Chapter 26: An Empty Homecoming 209

Chapter 27: The Call 216

Reflection 221

Chapter 28: A New Beginning 222

Chapter 29: Defining Us 227

Reflection 239

Chapter 30: New Directions 240

Reflection 246

Conclusion 247

About the Author 283

Chapter 1: A New Dawn in Douala

As the day started in Douala, my life was about to change in ways I couldn't imagine. The people who raised me had set the stage for everything to come. Our home was filled with the stories and lessons that would guide me as I stepped into a world that was beginning to shift around me.

****

My journey begins in Cameroon, a country rich in heritage and diversity in West Africa, just below the equator. Often called Africa in miniature, it includes a variety of climates, such as coastlines, deserts, mountains, rainforests, and savannas. This land is home to many ethnic groups and languages, making it unique. Douala, the largest city and economic capital, is a coastal metropolis and a key gateway. It plays an essential role in Central Africa's trade and culture, highlighting Cameroon's strategic importance.

The bustling markets were filled with vendors, clamoring for attention, and customers engaged in relentless negotiations, while the tempting aromas of grilled fish and sweet plantains filled the air. The nearby Atlantic Sea added a salty breeze to the experience. People loved Ndolé, a green stew made from leafy vegetables and served with plantains or rice. Puff-puff, a popular snack with a crispy exterior and a sweet interior, seemed to be sold at every tent. Delicious skewers of grilled soya, coated in spicy sauce sizzled at street stands, and the aroma of roasted corn on the cob scents the atmosphere. Even the rain added a refreshing odor on humid days.

My mother, Marthe, and her siblings lived in a small, steel-supported ranch-style house, elevated to avoid frequent flooding. The wooden walls were rotten and weak, and the floor resembled damaged pavement full of holes. The aluminum roof, long past its prime, allowed water to seep through the entire house during rainstorms.

My grandmother, Sen, my grandfather, Mahend, and their five children, Baboulek, Régine, Dieudonné, Annette, and Marthe, stayed in that home. During frequent rainfall, Marthe, Baboulek, and Annette would scramble with buckets, expertly catching and disposing of water—a routine they had mastered. My grandmother often shared memories, describing life before I was born.

"Cara," my grandmother would say to me, her eyes persistent as if reliving the memories, "We used to run around with those buckets, trying to keep the house from flooding. Mahend would always joke, saying we were practicing for a race, but those days were tough." I could still hear her voice as she continued. "One night, the heavy rain felt like the skies had opened. We moved from one area to another, trying to keep the water at bay. But despite it all, we found a moment to laugh and stay closely-knit. We were determined to make it through, and we did."

Each family member had a distinct role. Sen, a devoted stay-at-home spouse, focused on nurturing her children and supporting her husband, Mahend, a pastor at a local Protestant church. In Cameroon, religious centers serve as venues for worship and hubs for social interaction, playing an essential role in the cultural and social fabric. This includes a range of faiths, including Protestantism, Catholicism, Islam, and Indigenous beliefs. Mahend's responsibilities extended beyond his immediate family to the entire society. He spent his days preparing sermons, visiting parishioners, and coordinating religious and community activities. Every Sunday, dressed in their finest, the kin joined the congregation, where Mahend's compelling messages attracted people from the region.

Sen created a welcoming home, rising early each day to prepare breakfast—bread, tea, or porridge—before the children headed to school. Meticulous about cleanliness, she kept their dwelling in good order. On weekends, she organized family cleaning, assigning tasks such as sweeping, and hand-washing clothes. Her small vegetable plot in the yard supplied fresh produce for their meals. It was also a place where people gathered for tasty food and laughter. Two frequent visitors were Bachot, who lived two miles away, and had dropped out of high school, and Samuel, the next-door neighbor.

Baboulek, the eldest, was a protective and responsible figure, who fetched water from the well before school, ensuring enough for the day. He also handled repairs around the house, using his skills to fix leaks and patch walls. Everyone admired his industrious nature and vital duty.

Dieudonné, known for his adventurous spirit and curious mind, was always ready to learn and explore. He often ventured into the nearby woods, returning with exciting finds and tales of his adventures. One day, he discovered an unusual plant he believed had medicinal properties. Regardless of his siblings' skepticism, Dieudonné continued researching its potential uses. His enthusiasm for life spread joy to everyone around him, even during tough times when resources were scarce, and their fragile home required constant upkeep. His ventures often led to creative solutions for everyday problems, such as turning a broken bucket into a makeshift water carrier.

With her kind nature and nurturing spirit, Régine cared for her youngest siblings like a second mother. She had a talent for calming tempers and resolving conflicts, providing a soothing presence during the trying moments they often faced. Régine frequently organized games for her siblings, teaching them songs and dances to lift their spirits. She also took on the psychological labor of easing her siblings during storms, crafting bedtime stories to distract them from the rain battering their home.

Annette, a quiet and reflective person, found solace in reading and storytelling. She entertained the family with narratives from books and her imagination, offering a much-needed escape from daily life. Anette's tales combined local folklore with her creations. One of her favorites was about a courageous girl based in a village like theirs, who embarked on a quest to find magical flowers, that could bring rain during a drought. She shared these during the dry season when crops desperately needed water. Her stories captivated her loved ones, transporting them to distant lands, and making her the most beloved storyteller in the family.

The fifth child, Marthe, was shy and sweet, often quiet and reserved. Her warm nature and kind heart endeared her to everyone around. The house usually had to make do with what little they had. During one heavy rainy season, severe water damage made their home almost uninhabitable. She helped her mother and siblings clear the water seeped into their home overnight. Marthe stayed composed, offering quiet words of encouragement to her younger siblings. "We'll get through this," she would say softly, her voice steady while fighting the cold and tiredness.

The following morning, Marthe and her siblings followed their routine. They woke early to the soft light of dawn filtering through their windows. Before leaving for their destinations, they gathered for a simple breakfast. The youngest, Marthe, prepared for school, noticeably fell behind her siblings as they bid cheerful goodbyes. Making sure she was undetected; she slipped off in another direction. Unknown to both families, Marthe and Bachot would secretly meet and walk to school together, and they were involved in a more profound relationship than her family had known.

After departing from Bachot, she began feeling unwell. When the lunch hour arrived, she decided to stay in class despite the kitchen preparing her favorite meal of grilled fish, plantain, and spicy sauce. That afternoon, overcome with nausea, she had a difficult time concentrating. Marthe realized something was terribly wrong. The sensation intensified, prompting her to leave early and go home. When she arrived, she went straight to her room and lay down, knowing these ill sensations differed from any she had felt before.

Over the coming days, Sen noticed Marthe's change in behavior and asked, "Marthe, you've been distant lately. Is everything all right?" Marthe attributed it to schoolwork pressures and extracurricular activities. Sen accepted this explanation but remained concerned.

As Marthe's condition worsened, Sen confronted her more sternly. "Marthe, I need you to be honest with me. What is going on?" Marthe could no longer maintain the facade. With tears streaming down her face, she confessed to being pregnant and revealed that Bachot was the father.

Sen's expression turned pale. "My dear," she said softly, her voice a mix of concern and resignation, "You know your father, the pastor, will react differently to this news. We need to keep this between us. We need to figure out what to do next, but I need you to promise me not to tell anyone else until we devise a plan."

Marthe, tearful and overwhelmed, promised to keep the secret. Sen embraced her tightly, offering comfort as she wrestled with the situation's complexity. They understood that navigating their community's social and religious expectations would be challenging, with severe repercussions and fears of bringing shame to their household.

In Cameroon, individuals must be twenty-one years old to be considered adults. Marthe was younger than this age requirement, so she was considered a minor under Cameroonian law. This meant that Bachot's association with her was deemed a criminal offense, heightening the gravity of the situation.

If the pregnancy were to become known, her family would face immense ridicule from the community. Grappling with shock, Sen had to consider a solution for a stable future for Marthe and the child. Marriage, even at her young age, would be a solution that would preserve dignity. But not to Bachot, a man with little to offer. Samuel, the neighbor across the street, was an honest and diligent worker with a supportive family. Sen believed he would be an excellent husband for Marthe. She shared her plan with Marthe, who saw the benefits of implicating Samuel. They consented to frame him by misrepresenting evidence of the affair and concocting stories to protect the family's honor.

The morally dubious plan was driven by the urgent need to preserve their family's reputation and avoid severe judgment and potential repercussions. As the situation unfolded, Marthe and her mother prepared to face the fallout of their decision, fully aware of the consequences their actions might bring to them and Samuel. The weight of their deception tore deeply into their principles and moral conduct. With Marthe's changing physical appearance, solidifying this plan became more urgent.

Unseen during this discussion was Baboulek, who was silently lingering in the next room. He suspected something was very wrong with Marthe and needed to know. Upon hearing the extent of the truth, he was enraged and began formulating a plan to confront Bachot and bring him to justice. But this would be a secret he would hold to himself until an appropriate time, secretly honoring what he heard to be Marthe's will.

Pregnancy becomes a difficult condition to hide as time goes on despite wearing oversized clothing and avoiding the family wherever possible. Her admission to her father and the humiliation that ensued was yet another intolerable aspect of her situation. Mahend, reacting more like a religious zealot than grandfather, did little to shield her from the humiliation that came from, in his words, a lustful encounter. Although the blame was placed on Samuel, it would not ring true with the family or the community. The truth needed to be told.

One month before I was born, as the world was entering the Christmas season, tension continued to escalate due to the fallout from the pregnancy scandal, causing strain on the family. Because of the relentless efforts to frame Samuel, he and his family were forced to gather compelling evidence proving his innocence. Samuel presented this evidence to Mahend and Sen, firmly disproving any involvement.

The shame of that lie only multiplied the deep pity of her becoming an underaged mother. This anxiety may have contributed to Marthe's contractions intensifying, signaling that it was time for her to face the final stages of her pregnancy. Sen, witnessing the early signs of my arrival as Marthe's water broke on the kitchen floor.

Sen's command, "Get Bachot here right away," was fueled by the urgency to ensure Marthe received immediate medical attention. She realized her mistake as she spoke, knowing that her eldest child, Baboulek, was nearby and impatient to take charge. Her husband was busy preparing for church services, which allowed her son to step into a patriarchal role during this crisis.

Sen had made sure, some days back, that Bachot would know when Marthe was being taken to L'Hôpital Laquintinie, the primary hospital. He rushed there, determined to be present for the birth of his child, because avoiding this moment would be seen as cowardly. Baboulek and their father, Mahend, took immediate action, gathered the rest of their siblings, and sought help from concerned neighbors. Baboulek ran from house to house, explaining the urgency to neighbors who, quickly understanding the gravity, promised to help. The growing group focused on finding Bachot.

It was Christmas Eve, and as Douala fell into a peaceful quiet, Sen rushed Marthe to Laquintinie. The usual forty-three-minute commute seemed shorter due to the empty streets. Both Marthe and Sen were on edge and apprehensive during the trip. Marthe's cries of discomfort intensified with every bump, while Sen tried to comfort her.

Upon arrival, the cold, bright lights of the entrance contrasted sharply with the soft glow of the city and the warmth of her home. Although Marthe was in pain, she smiled at the Christmas decorations through the maternity ward, and the gentle sound of holiday music that played at the nurses' station. What had seemed like a burden, now felt like a Christmas gift as she prepared to welcome her child into the world.

During the delivery, Marthe's agony seemed to stretch time, with each contraction intensifying. The medical team focused on ensuring a safe delivery, while her family frantically searched for Bachot. Sen approached a nurse to inquire about Marthe's progress, and she shared that the delivery would be imminent.

Sen realized she had a limited window of opportunity. She knew they would arrive shortly at the facility, so she approached the group with a fabricated story, claiming she had overheard that Bachot had been seen at their house looking for Marthe. This deception was intended to mislead them, preventing interference with Bachot during this critical time. Her clan followed the misguided information, focusing on finding him; she remained in the delivery room, each second counting towards the arrival of the new life that would shift the family dynamics forever.

The plan succeeded as they left and returned to Bessengué to search for him. The drive back was heavy with silence, with each person keen to resolve the escalating situation. Sen seized the opportunity to ensure she could stay in the delivery room.

She coordinated with a medical staff member named Sallie, who confirmed Bachot was outside and eager to participate in this moment.

Her mission was clear: guide Bachot to the room without arousing suspicion. She found him waiting outside the main entrance, called him over, and, with a firm voice, gave him careful instructions. She explained the layout and stressed the importance of moving quickly to avoid being seen. Bachot followed her, his anxiety tempered by the presence of Sen, which helped him stay focused.

Upon reaching the delivery room, Sen ensured Bachot entered quietly, offering him a note of encouragement before stepping away. Marthe's eyes reflected excitement and hope, as she prepared for the sentimental weight of the moment. The nurse checked her dilation and confirmed she was ready to deliver. The gynecologist guided Marthe calmly, preparing her for birth.

As the suffering was accentuated with powerful contractions, her cries filled the room. Sen and Bachot held her hands, and the focus remained on the baby's arrival. Following the doctor's instructions, Marthe made the final push, and the baby was born.

The nurse cleansed and assessed the newborn and then handed the baby to my mother. Later, Sen shared how small and fragile I looked, wrapped in a blanket that provided warmth and comfort. Bachot, with tears in his eyes, looked at his child with both exhaustion and joy. Sen cradled me, and Bachot whispered, "Welcome to the world." Then he turned to my mother and said, "Thank you for this gift." My mother smiled through her tears. "We did this together," she whispered. Sen touched Bachot's shoulder, showing pride and relief. "We need to be careful now," she murmured.

The seriousness of the situation became clear. My grandmother and mother tried to stay positive, but knew my time with my father was limited. Bachot kissed my forehead and expressed, "I must leave now, but I promise I'll return."

My mother, tearful, added, "I'll be waiting." Sen quickly planned the next steps. "We need to create a distraction," she said. She suggested finding a way to help Bachot escape safely. He smiled, kissed Sen on the cheek, and said, "Thank you for everything. Go now. We will oversee things here," Sen replied.

Bachot glanced at my mother and me before leaving. The kinship group from Bessengué realized they had been manipulated, and returned to the healthcare center. When they arrived, they discovered he had escaped. Bachot walked the streets of Douala, heading toward Nigeria, hoping for a future free from the risks in Cameroon.

Marthe's relatives hurried through the halls, yearning to uncover the situation. Marthe, recovering from childbirth, was surrounded by her loved ones. They looked at me, a tiny new baby, with love.

Marthe, her mother, and I were discharged three days later and left. Sen later told me my mom looked happy as they walked to the car. The commute home was peaceful, like the calm after a storm. The scent of herbs and tasty food was in the air at home. Marthe and her mother placed me in a crib, and the house was alive with cheerful conversation.

They cherished these moments, enjoying the simple pleasure of watching me, and feeling my tiny fingers. Each day was special. Marthe put her education on hold to care for me.

My grandfather baptized me, showing his acceptance of me as a child of God, not an illegitimate product of a careless union. In Cameroonian culture, baptism is a new beginning. My mother recognized the significance of the ceremony, marking a moment of spiritual renewal. However, just as we embraced this connection, an unexpected revelation shattered the peace that had settled over us.

A shocking revelation suddenly disrupted our peaceful lives. We discovered that my grandfather had been unfaithful, and fathered a child named Odile with another woman, called Flore during a visit to a church thirty miles away from Bessengué. This disclosure caused a family rift, leading my grandmother to distance herself from him. Inheriting over forty acres of land in Yaoundé, she decided to make a fresh start, and began planning a trip there, intending to take me and my mother.

My Aunt, Annette, abruptly left one day, without any explanation. Her disappearance left us in confusion and worry, as we never heard from her again. Her absence added to the upheaval, amplifying our emotions.

My grandfather chose to leave my grandmother, and live with Flore, who was far from our family's previous home. This decision significantly impacted his loved ones.

My Uncle Baboulek secured a job in Yaoundé, marking a key milestone on his path to the future.

My Aunt Régine, filled with joy, announced her engagement to a promising surgeon named Komo, and followed him to embark on a new life in Ékounou.

In the home my grandmother left behind, my Uncle Dieudonné invited his fiancé Delphine to move in with him.

The remnants of our past remained, now joined by the sound of new aspirations.

Reflection

Strength in Adversity:

Thinking back to the early days of our life in Douala, I'm struck by how resourceful we were, especially during the relentless rainy season. The image of my mother and her siblings, scrambling with buckets to keep the house dry is more than just a memory; it is a testament to our ability to find strength and humor in the face of adversity. It reminds me that surviving the storm is about resilience, and finding ways to laugh and stay connected.

The Power of Small Acts:

My grandmother, Sen, waking up early each morning, to prepare breakfast for her children may seem like a simple, everyday act, but it was through these small, consistent actions that she built a home filled with love and stability. It reminds me that the small acts of care we offer to those around us are the building blocks of a robust and nurturing environment. Sometimes, it is the simplest gestures that have the most profound impact.

The Unseen Struggles:

As a child, I didn't fully understand the challenges my grandparents faced. The weak walls of the house, the constant struggle to keep it from flooding, and the lack of resources were all part of daily life. Now, I see how much strength it took for them to keep things steady. It reminds me that the most brutal battles are often fought quietly, behind the scenes.

The Nuances of Relationships:

The dynamics were filled with unspoken emotions, and hidden truths. For instance, Marthe's secret relationship with Bachot was something few indeed recognized. It made me reflect on how connections often have deeper layers that aren't immediately visible. This reminds me to approach relationships with empathy, knowing there might be more beneath the surface than we realize.

Tradition and Transformation:

My grandfather baptizing me, despite the circumstances of my birth, stands as a powerful symbol. This act taught me the importance of continuity and identity, even as life changes. It also serves as a reminder, that practices can evolve to embrace new meanings.

The Weight of Our Choices:

My grandmother's actions, especially her determination to protect Marthe and handle the challenges, remind me of how our actions influence those around us. What she did shape us profoundly, showing how even the toughest moments can ripple through the lives of others

Additional Elements:

Historical or Cultural Context:

Thinking about these experiences, I also considered the broader context of life in Cameroon during that time. Our story is connected to the country's deep traditions and the importance of family and social expectations. As we navigated these cultural nuances, I greatly appreciated the strength my family showed.

Personal Growth and Perspective:

Looking back, my perspective on this event has changed. As a child, I saw things more simply, but with time and experience, I've come to see the deeper layers of our struggles. I hope you find growth as you consider your life stories.

Universal Themes:

The themes of family, perseverance, and the subtleties of relationships are not unique to my story—they are universal. I hope you find echoes of your experiences, and draw strength from how my family navigated their challenges.

Questions for the Reader to Consider:

Have you ever had to find strength, in the face of adversity? What small acts of kindness have shaped your life? My family's experiences might mirror your own, offering lessons you can draw from them.

Hints of What is to Come:

Our journey began with the strength, and love my family showed in Douala. These moments laid the foundation for everything that came next. As you read on, you'll see how these early times shaped us, and led to the victories that followed.

Chapter 2: Seeds of Resilience

We left the city behind as we traveled to Yaoundé, where my grandmother, Sen, planned to turn barren land, into a place full of life. Together, we were learning the rhythms of the land, working toward something meaningful. The scenery gradually changed from city streets, to open countryside lined with tall trees. The road offered brief shade, as the leaves formed a canopy overhead. The long drive marked the beginning of her work, to transform the neglected farm into something that could support us all.

****

Upon reaching the property, Sen was met with a sight that might have discouraged many. The estate lay in disrepair, overrun with weeds, and the soil appeared tired and dry. Yet, where others saw ruin, she saw potential. This land, a gift from her late aunt, was a blank canvas for her vision of renewal and prosperity.

Determined to revive the farm, Sen quickly assembled a team of twelve, skilled workers, each contributing their expertise. Mbenge, the agronomist, revitalized the soil. Ntemba, the irrigation specialist, designed a system to keep the crops well-watered. Essi, the carpenter, repaired the farm's structures, and built storage sheds. The remaining workers, each with unique talents, played crucial roles in planting and harvesting.

The first crops were sown in March, in harmony with the Cameroonian farming season, which welcomed the rains. Soon, the farm became known for its abundance and diversity. Rows of lettuce, tomatoes, peppers, and celery flourished alongside banana and plantain trees. Coffee and cacao plants, with their lush green foliage, promised future harvests of rich beans. Maize and spinach thrived under the warm sun, while fruit trees bore oranges, mangoes, and papayas, all creating a rich produce tapestry.

Over time, the fields prospered, turning into successful enterprises. Sen, now a respected figure in this new community, sold the produce at local trading centers. The farm supported our family, provided jobs, and became crucial to the local economy and social life.

The farming season ended with the harvest, which showed my grandmother's hard work and dedication to the land. The once-abandoned field is now used for others, supporting those around us. Sen's efforts in farming made her a respected figure, and she was known for her wisdom.

When this busy season ended, life at home became more relaxed, with the workers on a well-deserved break. She shifted her focus to everyday moments with us. Each day began in the early light of dawn. Rising early, she tiptoed, already in tune with the day ahead. My mother, attentive to my needs, wrapped me in a traditional cloth, keeping me close to her. At 12 months old, I was still too young to walk alone, but I was always near them.

We took a 20-minute walk from our new home to the farmland. The path led through greenery with the morning mist clinging to the leaves. My grandmother pointed out various plants and trees along the way, sharing what she knew. These walks were more than just a trip to the farm; they were learning moments.

"See that tree, child?" she would say, pointing to a towering mango tree. "It stands tall because its roots are deep. In life, you must never forget to stay grounded. The storms may come, but if your roots are strong, you will not fall."

At the farm, a small shed offered shade and a place for me to rest and play, while my mother and grandmother tended to the last of the harvest or checked on the animals. Nearby, a clear river flowed gently, providing refreshment and sustenance. My mother often bathed in the river, washing away the sweat of the morning's labor. On some days, they would fish, skillfully pulling in the day's catch, which we later enjoyed for dinner.

Though physically tiring, the return walk always brought satisfaction. The cool breeze of the late afternoon offered a welcome reprieve from the sun's warmth as we returned home, the day's work done.

Evenings in our home were times of quiet joy and reflection. Dinner was a simple yet hearty affair, often consisting of fresh produce from the farm, and the fish caught earlier in the day. The scent spread through the room, while we sat around the table, lit by the soft glow of the oil lamp in our warm home.

After dinner, we gathered in the living room, a modest space rich with life. It was during these times that my grandmother's wisdom truly shone. She would tell us stories, using parables and sayings, each tale a carefully crafted lesson in life. Her voice was calm and steady, drawing us in with every word.

One evening, as we settled in for another of her stories, she began, "There was once a young girl who wanted to be the best at everything she did. She worked hard, but she never gave herself a moment to rest. One day, she fell ill and could not do anything at all. That is when she learned that life is not just about running fast, but knowing when to slow down. Child, remember this: there is a time to work, and a time to rest. Do both wisely."

Another night, as the crickets sang outside and the stars dotted the sky, she shared, "A man planted a tree in his garden, hoping it would bear fruit quickly. He watered it every day, but the tree grew slowly. Impatient, he forced it to grow faster, by pulling on its branches. But in his haste, he broke the tree. In life, you must have patience. Some things take time, and you must nurture them gently."

Her stories often reflected the values she held dear—hard work, honesty, and the importance of staying true to oneself. Lessons were part of our daily lives. Sen's words were firm, yet profound, and they stayed with us, long after the last word was spoken.

Our little family found peace in these quiet moments, with the day's work behind us, and the night stretching ahead. Our bonds grew stronger each day, shaped by the love, wisdom, and resilience my grandmother so effortlessly embodied.

As the days went on, my grandmother's wisdom became the cornerstone of our evenings. After a long day at the farm, we eagerly gathered around her, ready for the tales she spun with grace. One evening, after the sun had dipped below the horizon, and the farm rested quietly in twilight, she began another one.

"Once, there was a farmer who had two pots," she started, her voice warm and inviting, drawing us into her world. "Every day, he would carry water from the river to his home. One of the pots was perfect, and it always held its water to the brim. The other pot had a crack in it, and by the time the farmer reached his home, it was only half full."

Letting the words settle in our minds, she stopped. My mother held me close, while I listened intently, and understood the importance of her words, even at my young age.

"One day, the cracked pot spoke to the farmer, full of shame. 'I'm sorry,' it said. 'Because of my flaw, you don't get the full amount of water you work so hard to carry.'

"But the farmer," she continued, her voice dropping to a whisper, "he smiled at the pot and said, 'Look at the path we take to my home. Do you see the flowers on your side? As we walked, I planted seeds along the path, and you watered them daily. Thanks to you, my home is full of beauty and fragrance. Your flaw is not a weakness; it is a gift.'"

As the story ended, she looked at us with deep, knowing eyes. "Child, never be ashamed of what you think are your flaws. They are what make you unique. They can bring beauty into the world, in ways you may not see at first. Remember, it is not perfection that makes us strong, but how we use what we have."

The story lingered in the air, its message clear and comforting. In these moments, surrounded by her strength and love, I learned the true power of resilience and hope.

In the quiet moments of the day, my grandmother would often recount tales that were more than just stories—they were life lessons woven into our daily existence. One that stayed with me, was about a man consumed by greed. As she said, a man came to a well, a vital water source for the entire village. Instead of taking what he needed and leaving the rest for others, he drank until the well was dry. To make matters worse, when he had his fill, he defiled the well by urinating into it, thinking only of himself.

But as he walked away, smug with the belief that he had outsmarted everyone, karma took its course. He tripped and fell into the very well he had polluted, and there he remained, stuck in the filth of his own making. My grandmother would pause after this part of the story, letting the weight of the lesson sink in. "Greed," she would say, "is a trap you set for yourself."

Her stories went beyond warnings about greed. She believed sincerely in the value of arduous work, and the idea that you reap what you sow. This wasn't just a saying for her; it was a principle she lived by, and taught us all. She would tell me that if I wanted more in life, I had to put in the effort. "Nothing comes easy. You must get up in the morning, knock on doors, and hustle. Life doesn't give out rewards—you earn them."

Her commitment to treating others with kindness and respect matched this belief in perseverance. "Treat others as you would like to be treated," she would remind me often, "but don't just sit back and wait for things to happen. You have to keep moving, pushing forward, and never stop."

Through her guidance, my grandmother taught me the value of hard work, and the importance of staying true to yourself, no matter the circumstances. These teachings shaped the person I would become, long after they were shared.

Life on the farm settled into a familiar routine as I approached 18 months. Mornings still began with the rituals my grandmother had established, and evenings ended with her timeless teachings. Only a watchful eye could detect the subtle changes around us.

Marthe started spending more time with her friends. Their connection, once distant, began to flourish again. Through these renewed friendships, she met Thomas, a man different from those she had known before—older, with a quiet confidence that intrigued her. He was a schoolteacher with a gentle demeanor, and a strong presence. Always respectful, he greeted my grandmother with a slight bow and a warm smile. But beneath his politeness, a charm drew my mother closer to him.

Their meetings started innocently, with conversations shared over the fence, while Marthe tended the garden or helped with chores. But as time passed, their connection deepened. He became a regular presence at our home, often joining the evening gatherings. His visits became more frequent, and his presence more noticeable each day.

Sen observed the changes with both concern and understanding. She knew Marthe was facing a crucial decision, torn between her role as a mother and her desire for a different life. The draw of her old life, and the allure of new romance began to create a distance between my mother and me, a separation that Sen feared would only grow, affecting us all.

After a day at the farm, Sen found herself alone with Marthe. The house was quiet, with only the sounds of the night. Seizing the moment, Sen spoke softly, sharing her thoughts and experiences.

"Marthe," she began, "I see the changes in you, how your eyes light up when you're with your friends when you talk about Thomas. It is natural to want more from life, to reclaim what you feel you have lost. But remember, you have a child now, and that child needs you more than ever. You have responsibilities that cannot be set aside."

My mother looked down, the weight of my grandmother's words settling over her. She knew the truth in them, but the call of her past, and the allure of her newfound independence were strong. She nodded, but her heart was conflicted, caught between the life she had and the life she wanted.

Marthe began to spend more time with Thomas and her friends, and less time at home with us. The farm, once central to her life, now seemed like a reminder of something she was leaving behind. Gradually, the presence I had always known began to fade. Missed meals and late returns became more common, and she was clearly searching for something our home could no longer offer.

Sen noticed the shift deeply. The connection with her daughter was weakening. She knew she couldn't stop Marthe from pursuing her new life, but worried about what it meant for me. After Marthe left with Thomas, for what she said would be a short visit to the city, Sen sat by the fire, worry settling in. She knew deep down that Marthe might not return. This understanding weighed on her like a cold mist.

When Marthe didn't return that night, Sen wasn't surprised. She had prepared herself for this moment, even as she hoped it wouldn't come. Rising early, she prepared for the day and carried on as usual. But she knew things had changed. Life would never be the same. It was evident that my mother had left, not just for a day or two, but for good. She had chosen a different path, one that didn't include me. Sen took me in her arms and held me close. She would raise me as her own with love.

Losing my mother left a mark on both of us, one that would take years to heal. Her absence shaped who I became just as much as the love and care Sen provided. Life on the farm continued as time passed, but a new challenge emerged—something we couldn't have predicted. Sen began to feel a tiredness that wouldn't go away, and a slight yellowing appeared in her eyes. At first, these signs were dismissed as mere exhaustion. But soon, it was clear that something was wrong. Sen, who had always been strong, started to weaken. Her skin turned yellow, and her movements slowed. She tried to continue as if nothing had changed, but the signs were there. At two and a half years old, I was too young to understand what was happening. The lightness in our home faded, replaced by worries that lingered. Sen's illness soon began to show in me as well.

At two and a half years old, I was too young to grasp what was happening entirely, but I sensed the change. Worry replaced the usual warmth in our home, as Sen's illness became more apparent. Before long, I, too, began to show symptoms, marking a shift in our daily lives.

A fever took hold, leaving me weak and drained. My head throbbed, and keeping my eyes open became a struggle. Sen, even as she faced her challenges, cared for me. She cooled my forehead, spoke softly to comfort, and held me close through the pain.

Over time, my condition worsened, and I grew weaker. My grandmother, desperate to help, reached out to our neighbors. They brought food and medicine, but nothing seemed to work. I was soon too weak to respond.

Seeing our dire state, one of the neighbors took it upon herself to contact my uncle, Baboulek. He had moved to Ngaoundéré, a city far to the north, and had established a life there. The news of his grandmother's illness, and my worsening condition reached him, and without hesitation, he set off for Yaoundé.

When Baboulek arrived, he found the home he once knew transformed. His mother, who had always been his anchor, was lying in bed, her skin pale, and her eyes heavy with exhaustion. Nearby, I lay weak and barely conscious, struggling to hold on.

He knelt by his mother's side, gently taking her hand and asking what had happened. She explained the days of struggle, the efforts to care for me, and the search for relief that never came.

"I have done all I can," she said, "But she's getting worse. I don't know what else to do."

In response to the words, I fainted and collapsed onto the floor. Seeing me lying there, my uncle acted quickly, lifting me and feeling the heat radiating from my body. There was no time to waste.

"We need to get her to the hospital," Baboulek said, his voice filled with urgency. "She's too weak. We can't wait any longer."

Though hesitant to let me go, my grandmother knew there was no other choice. She allowed my uncle to take me to the hospital. The ride felt like it would never end, with the strain growing as time dragged on.

When we arrived at the hospital, my condition was quickly assessed. The diagnosis was meningitis. The doctor explained that the infection had reached my brain and spine, and it might be too late to save me. The treatment was swift. They performed a lumbar puncture, drawing fluid from my spine to relieve the pressure. The procedure was difficult and left me crying out, but it was necessary to save my life.

Antibiotics were administered, hoping to stop the infection. I stayed in the hospital for days, with my condition under close watch. Slowly, the fever began to break, and the pain that had overwhelmed me started to ease. Showing signs of improvement, it wasn't long before I was allowed to return home, though I would need to continue my medication for some time.

When my uncle brought me back home, it was evident that things had changed. My grandmother, weakened by jaundice, struggled to care for both of us, feeling the toll it had taken on her. Sitting down with her, my uncle spoke softly but firmly, "She can't stay here," he said. "You are too weak to take care of her. I will take her with me, to Ngaoundéré. She needs to be somewhere she can be properly looked after."

Even though it pained her to let me go, my grandmother knew it was the right decision. With tears in her eyes, she placed a hand on my uncle's arm. "Take care of her."

My uncle gathered my belongings, and prepared to take me to my new home in Ngaoundéré. As I left, I looked back at my grandmother, standing in the doorway, her eyes conveying everything she felt. It was the last time I would see her before we left, but her presence would remain with me, a guiding light in the years to come.

The trip to Ngaoundéré began, leaving me unsure of what lay ahead, but something in me hoped for the care and safety I needed. I clung to that hope, holding on as tightly as I did to the memories of the life I was leaving behind.

.

Reflection

What I went through was more than just a trip. It marked a shift from turmoil, to peace, and doubt, to new beginnings. The changing environments reflected our growth, showing that even the hardest roads can lead to change. My grandmother's ability to look beyond immediate struggles, and see a better future was a powerful example of wisdom. She led by bringing out the best in everyone around her, showing that true success is built on collective efforts. These lessons of seeing potential, embracing change, working together, and finding strength in the community have shaped how I approach every challenge in life, always seeking greater possibilities.

Chapter 3: The New Beginning in Ngaoundéré

Have you ever packed up your life and moved to a place you had never been? That is precisely what happened when we set off for Ngaoundéré. Unfamiliar faces, new routines, and many surprises were waiting. Buckle up—this is where the adventure begins.

****

I felt both excited and nervous on the trip to Ngaoundéré. My uncle Baboulek made sure I was comfortable. He talked about the new place that would soon be home.

Ngaoundéré, nestled in the Adamawa region of Cameroon, boasts a captivating and diverse landscape. Rolling hills, and expansive plateaus, offering breathtaking views that stretch to the horizon. The city's elevation provides a cooler climate, a refreshing change from the humidity of Yaoundé. The countryside is a serene oasis, adorned with traditional Fulani huts and extensive cattle ranches, reflecting the deep-rooted culture of the Fulani people. Meandering rivers and streams with clear, glistening waters add tranquility to the scene.

Upon our arrival, the staff welcomed us warmly. The villa was on a slope, offering a wide view. It was more than just a residence; it represented my uncle's achievements. The house was vast and grand, with seven bedrooms and five bathrooms. A towering gate at the entrance ensured our security. The team, which included guards, housekeepers, a chef, and a chauffeur, worked seamlessly to keep everything running smoothly.

My Uncle was highly regarded as the head of Ngaoundéré 's treasury, and a successful entrepreneur. Behind the villa, the garden featured a guest house, a chicken coop, and spaces for goats and cows. The eggs produced were well-known in the region, and milk from the livestock contributed to the household's income. The property was always busy, showing his success; his wife, Elga, welcomed me with open arms. She was chic and elegant, standing about five feet six inches tall, with light skin, and a sophisticated appearance. Their son, Alain, a skinny, tan little boy of four and a half years with well-groomed short hair, ran to greet me. "Welcome home, baby sister," he said with a broad smile, hugging me tightly. From that moment, my uncle became "Papa," and Elga became "Mama." In my eyes, they were my actual parents.

Our time at the villa was a daily gift. Breakfasts were diverse, with fruits, vegetables, eggs, and cheeses filling the table. The chef prepared a feast for the senses, with each dish carefully crafted and presented. Afternoons after school were spent doing homework, playing with Alain, or riding bicycles around the spacious property. Occasionally, children from the neighborhood joined us, but we rarely left the grounds. The villa was so large that there was always plenty of space to explore, and enjoy within its walls.

In the evenings, we prayed together, and then watched the news. Afterward, we gathered in another room, where Uncle Baboulek shared stories and anecdotes. These narratives, blending wisdom and entertainment, reflected the cherished values and lessons he wished to impart.

One of his treasured tales was about a young boy determined to build the tallest tower in his village. The boy worked tirelessly, stacking stones higher and higher, but each time he neared completion, a strong wind would knock the building down. Frustrated but undeterred, he tried repeatedly, learning more with each attempt. Eventually, he realized that the foundation's strength was the key to success. With this new understanding, he built the sturdiest tower in the village, which stood for many years. My Uncle would remind us that the lesson was about the importance of creating a solid foundation in life, whether in relationships, work, or personal goals.

Another story he often shared was about a man who sought the secret to happiness. The man traveled everywhere, meeting wise elders and searching for answers, but each piece of advice seemed to fail. Finally, tired and discouraged, the man returned home. Sitting under a tree, he noticed a small bird singing joyfully despite the stormy weather. He knew joy came from inside, not outside. My uncle often said real happiness comes from within, not from what happens around us.

One evening, he shared a tale about a merchant known for his honesty and integrity. A customer accused the merchant of cheating but stood firm, knowing he had done nothing wrong. Over time, the truth became known, and the merchant's reputation for honesty grew even more. "Always keep your word," my uncle would advise, "because your integrity is worth more than gold."

These stories were a special part of our nights. They were more than tales; they were lessons. My uncle's calm voice shared his experience, and I felt close to his values as he spoke.

Our routine at the villa set in. Our chef prepared breakfast each morning with fruits, vegetables, eggs, and cheese. Afternoons were spent doing homework, playing with Alain, and riding bikes around the large property. Sometimes, other kids from the neighborhood joined us, but we mostly stayed within the villa's grounds. The estate had plenty of space for us to explore and enjoy. Yet, behind the scenes, things were changing. A different story unfolded, with secrets and a growing distance between my uncle and Elga. My uncle didn't see that Elga's affection was drifting. His demanding job often kept him away, leaving space for Victor, a man who was more than an acquaintance, to step in. The home, once stable, started to change.

One evening, after a long trip, my uncle sensed a change. The warmth was gone, and there was tension as he entered the living room. The villa felt different as the truck pulled into the driveway. The engine's rumble signaled that something was wrong. Just back from a long journey, my uncle stood in the doorway, confused and angry. Elga stormed out of the house, not calm anymore. She went to the gate and told the guard to open it, but a truck was idling outside. Victor was behind the wheel, his presence unwanted.

My uncle called out, 'What are you doing?' as he followed her, trying to understand. 'Who is this man?' Without answering at first, she continued packing. 'Yes,' she eventually said. 'His name is Victor, and he's been more of a partner to me than you ever were.'

'This is our home,' my uncle pleaded. 'This is where we built our life and raised our children. You can't just throw that away.' There was a brief silence before she said, 'I'm sorry, Baboulek, but I've decided I am leaving tonight.'

Victor entered the house as she spoke, adding to the tension. My uncle turned to him, fists clenched, but before he could act, Elga stepped between them. 'Don't, Baboulek,' she warned. 'This is over. You need to let me go.' The argument went on as their relationship unraveled. My uncle, exhausted, tried to reason with her to keep the family together, but Elga was firm. More of her belongings were loaded into the truck, marking the end of this part of our lives.

She turned to my uncle, who stood in the driveway, and said, 'Goodbye, Baboulek. Take care, Alain.' Then she got into the truck beside Victor. They drove off Without another word, leaving him alone outside as the truck's sound faded.

As the taillights vanished into the night, a silence fell over the villa. My uncle stood there, taking in what had just happened. The woman he loved and built a life with left, and she was not returning. The finality of it was overwhelming. Weeks passed, and the villa became a place of sorrow and confusion. My uncle threw himself into his work to cope with the pain, but the emptiness stayed no matter how much he worked. The villa constantly reminded him of everything he had lost. Alain and I adjusted to the new normal, but Elga's absence was always felt. My uncle took on both roles, ensuring we felt loved and secure. In the years that followed, we never heard from Elga again. She vanished from our lives as quickly as she entered. The process was swift and uncontested. Now living with Victor, Elga wanted nothing from my uncle—no alimony, no property. She just wanted a clean break and a fresh start with the man she had chosen. And just like that, our time together was over. The pains of Elga's departure faded as time passed, but the experience stayed with us. We emerged stronger, bound by what we went through. The house became a place where new memories were created. It wasn't the size of the home or the wealth that mattered but the connection we shared within its walls. That became the foundation for building our future.

<u>Reflection</u>

Going to Ngaoundéré was more than just changing places. It was finding new ways to fit in. We learned that changes could bring new starts and growth. My uncle will show us the demanding work and support he has given our family. Watching my uncle handle his job and home showed me what he taught me. He indicated that good leaders are not just in charge but also there for others no matter what. Elga's leaving showed me that not all changes are reasonable. It taught me that relationships can end and that being strong is essential when things are tough. We should appreciate the people who stay and find support in lasting friendships.

Chapter 4: A Growing Family and New Beginnings

Are you ready for a whirlwind of change? In this chapter, our villa transforms into a hub with new faces, bringing laughter, love, and surprises. We'll explore the ups and downs of an expanding household, discovering how even unexpected twists can lead to growth and new adventures.

****

After Elgar left, life at home began to settle into a new normal. My uncle focused on rebuilding our household, continued his work, pursued his Ph.D., and prepared for the exams needed to become a diplomat, hoping to serve in London. Despite his many responsibilities, he always emphasized what truly mattered.

Recognizing the need for support, my uncle invited Pauline, my 16-year-old aunt from Puma, to live with us. She brought Nelly, a five-year-old cousin, whose parents had abandoned her. Their arrival brought significant changes to our household.

Pauline, petite with light skin and a quiet demeanor, had an air of maturity beyond her years due to the challenges she had faced growing up. On the other hand, Nellie was a bright-eyed, lively child, full of curiosity and energy. Their addition to our home brought warmth and completeness that had been missing since Elga's departure.

The transition was seamless, as my uncle was always a source of stability and care. He welcomed Pauline and Nellie warmly, ensuring they felt safe from the moment they arrived. What once felt empty after Elgar left was now full of life again, with the presence of more family bringing new energy to our home.

We quickly adjusted to having them with us. Pauline took on a caring role, helping with chores, looking after us, and assisting with homework. This eased my uncle's mind.

Mornings were busy with activities. Breakfast was pleasant, with Pauline helping the maids and Nelly often sharing her dreams from the night before. After breakfast, Alain and I would head to school while they left for school later.

In the afternoons, we would return home to find Pauline and Nellie waiting for us. Homework was always the first order of business, but the afternoons were ours to enjoy once that was done. We would play in the gardens, ride bicycles, or sometimes sit under the shade of the trees, listening to Pauline's stories from Puma. Like my uncle, she had a talent for storytelling, and her tales of life in the village fascinated us.

After dinner, which the chef always prepared with great care, we would pray in the living room. This was followed by our nightly ritual of watching the news with my uncle, informing us about the world beyond our home. During these quiet moments, he often shared his own stories and anecdotes, passing on the wisdom he had gained.

One evening, after the news, my uncle shared a story about a young boy who dreamed of becoming a diplomat, just like him. The boy worked hard, studied diligently, and overcame many obstacles to achieve his goal. Along the way, he learned that the accurate measure of success wasn't just in titles or accolades, but in the relationships he built, and the people he helped. The story resonated deeply with all of us, especially Pauline, who dreamed of one day making a difference in the world.

Another time, he told us about a wise elder who always spoke kindly, even to those who wronged him. When asked why he was always so gentle, the elder replied, "The words you speak are like seeds; they will grow into the garden of your life. I choose to plant seeds of kindness, for I wish to live in a garden of peace." This reminded us of the importance of our words and actions, a lesson that stayed long after the tale was told.

As we moved forward, our home became more than just a place to live. My uncle's presence brought the joy that had been missing. We were connected not just by blood, but by the experiences that had shaped us.

With my uncle's continued success in his career and his dreams of becoming a diplomat, we knew that changes were coming. Whatever the future held, we were ready to face it together.

One day, my uncle received two pieces of news that would change our lives again. First, he had passed the initial requirements for his dream of serving as a diplomat in London. It was an important step closer to his ambition, and the entire family rejoiced at the news. The possibility of moving to Europe was exciting and daunting, but we were all proud of his achievements.

However, the second piece of news was less joyous. He had been reassigned to a remote village called Ngok Mapubi, far from our life in Ngaoundéré. Though it was a setback in his plans for London, he accepted it calmly. He explained that sometimes life takes unexpected turns, but every experience has value, no matter how challenging.

The news of his new post reminded us of how unpredictable life can be. Though we cherished our time in Ngaoundéré, it was time to start anew. One evening, he gathered us to talk about the next steps.

The news of my uncle's reassignment lingered in the air, a reminder that life's journey is often unpredictable. As much as we cherished our life in Ngaoundéré, the time had come to embrace a new chapter. My Uncle, always the pillar of strength and optimism, gathered us together one evening to discuss the move.

We've been through a lot together," he began, his voice calm. "Now, we face another change. The move will be different, but if we stick together, we can make anywhere feel like home."

We listened closely to his words. We were both excited about the adventure ahead and sad about what we were leaving behind. The residence, with its gardens and the memories we created, will always hold a special place in our hearts. But he reminded us that home is not just about a location; it's where we find support and one another.

Packing became the focus at the villa. Pauline and Nellie helped, while Alain and I wondered what life in Ngok Mapubi might be like. My uncle, ever organized, made sure everything was ready. The staff exchanged farewells as they completed their final tasks.

The day we left felt quieter, as if the villa knew this was the end of an era. Packed bags, closed shutters, and covered furniture signaled it was time to go. We stood outside, ready to leave. My uncle took one last look at the home, then turned to us and said, 'Let's go. Our new adventure awaits.'

And with that, we set out for Ngok Mapubi, leaving behind Ngaoundéré and everything familiar. The drive took us through winding roads, symbolizing the changes we were ready to embrace. With each mile, we moved further from the past, carrying our memories and looking ahead to what Ngok Mapubi might offer.

Reflection

Pauline and Nellie's arrival changed everything. Their presence turned the villa from a quiet place into a lively home. Welcoming them showed how important it is to have people around us. My uncle's decision to bring them into our home was a gesture of kindness. It wasn't just about replacing Elga but about creating a place where everyone could belong. This choice reminded us that family is defined by the care and responsibility we give to each other.

Watching Pauline take on responsibility at such a young age taught me a lot. Her way of caring for others showed that leadership can emerge unexpectedly. Her actions reinforced the importance of looking out for those around us.

The routines that developed with Pauline and Nellie's arrival brought a new rhythm to our days. Shared moments, from breakfast to evening prayers, became the foundation of our lives. These practices created a sense of security and belonging, especially during the transition. My uncle's stories weren't just about the past; they were lessons he lived by and wanted to pass on. They showed how storytelling connects us to our roots and shapes the future.

His reassignment to Ngok Mapubi reminded us that life can change unexpectedly. It taught me that while we may plan and dream, we must sometimes adapt. His calm response to the news showed how important it is to see change as an opportunity to grow. Moving from Ngaoundéré to Ngok Mapubi showed that home is not just a place but a feeling created by the people around us. His actions during this time taught me that any place can become home.

Saying goodbye to Ngaoundéré meant leaving behind a part of our lives but also stepping into something new. The memories and lessons we gathered came with us. This change showed me that life moves forward, and we must move with it.

Chapter 5: Arrival in Ngok Mapubi - Changes and Challenges

Ngok Mapubi looked like a postcard on sunny days and starry nights. We thought we were trading city chaos for village peace, but we quickly learned that small-town life had its surprises. In a place where everyone knew your business, the calm exterior hid secrets ready to surface.

****

We moved from Ngaoundéré to Ngok Mapubi, a village in the Littoral region of Cameroon. The town was smaller but had its charm, with traditions and modernity. Many government officials lived there, including our new neighbors, like my uncle, who served the community. We settled into my uncle's new house. It wasn't as big as the home we left behind, but it was nice enough for us. The house had three bedrooms, three baths, a nice interior, a large backyard, and a colorful front porch.

Adjusting to life in a slower, peaceful environment took time. Each day began with familiar routines—prayers and breakfast—keeping a sense of normalcy despite the change. Even with the demands of his role as head of treasury, my uncle stayed committed to his work, managing community funds and building relationships with local officials. Pauline's help was essential in keeping our household stable.

Nellie, Alain, and I continued our studies and extracurricular activities, taking advantage of the village's opportunities. Now, in junior high, I was excited to make new friends and continue excelling in my education. My academic achievements, and involvement in the volleyball team, earned me the admiration of my peers. Sponsoring the team with my uncle's support allowed me to make a tangible difference, and the accomplishment was deeply fulfilling.

We made new friends in the neighborhood, growing and discovering more about ourselves. The joy of forming new bonds enriched our lives, though sometimes, the privilege of being dropped off in a magnificent car sparked jealousy among other students.

As we settled into daily life, my uncle's potential diplomatic role in London became more likely. He worked hard to prepare for the required tests, while managing his current duties. The possibility of moving to London meant leaving behind what we had just started to build.

During this time, my uncle met a schoolteacher named Susanne, who quickly became the object of his previously dormant desire. Because of that, intimacy began early in the relationship, which resulted in a pregnancy. They soon welcomed twins, Baboulek Jr. and Celine. Susanne initially kept her apartment, but eventually moved in with us. She naturally became part of our lives and fit into our household without effort.

However, this stability was short-lived. After just a few months, Susanne left with the twins and returned to her mother's house in Douala. The departure was abrupt, and came without a clear explanation. Pauline shared with me that there were whispers of disagreements between Susanne and my uncle in the days leading up to it. She mentioned that the pressure of blending families, the demands of raising twins, and perhaps unresolved issues from my uncle's past played a role in her decision. Though young and not privy to private conversations, I sensed the tension, the arguments behind closed doors, and the frustrations in my uncle's eyes.

I was left confused and wondering why two crucial women in my uncle's life chose to leave. The emptiness they left behind was complete, and while some reasons were hinted at, the whole story remained unclear.

Heartbroken, my uncle quickly connected with a young woman named Madeline, who lived 45 minutes away in a nearby village. He met her during one of his visits to drop off money at their small office. What began as casual interactions, grew into conversations, and their acquaintance turned into a friendship, then a love story.

Madeline brought joy to my uncle's life and, in turn, to our family. His trips and gifts reflected a deeper connection. My uncle's generosity toward her family showed his love. His happiness was clear to everyone who knew him, bringing a positive energy to our home.

For a time, their love story touched our lives. The household welcomed Madeline, who became a regular presence. Her visits brought new energy, and we looked forward to the future with optimism. However, my uncle's frequent absences left us managing the household on our own. Alain grew mean and hostile towards me, disrupting the peace. Pauline and I tried to keep things in order, but the tension was evident.

Alain's behavior started with small acts of defiance—ignoring requests, rolling his eyes, and muttering under his breath. Gradually, his actions became more severe. He would hide my belongings, sabotage my chores, and make sharp remarks whenever possible. The peace in our home crumbled as his behavior worsened. Pauline and I leaned on each other to manage, but the tension grew. His outbursts became frequent, often escalating into arguments. He began skipping school, staying out late, and challenging anyone who tried to guide him.

His behavior became clear through several incidents. He once locked me out of the house, leaving me stranded until Pauline returned. Another time, he ruined a birthday gift I had received, smirking as he watched my distress. These actions created an atmosphere of tension and disruption. The idea of Madeline joining our household came after discussions between her and my uncle focused on his behavior, and the need for support to help him get back on track.

I developed ways to cope, by paying close attention to his moods, and avoiding confrontations when possible. The hope that Madeline's presence might bring peace and safety to the house kept me going.

Looking for comfort, I turned to Pauline, who had become my confidant during this time. Her responses always reassured me that the situation was temporary, and that change was coming. 'It won't last forever,' she would say, helping me cope with the bullying.

Pauline's support was crucial. She listened to my concerns, and offered a perspective that gave me hope. She believed Madeline's presence could positively impact our household and help change Alain's behavior.

As the family processed the news, thoughts about the upcoming changes began. Discussions began about when and how Madeline would move in.

The time before Madeline's move was focused on getting ready. The family organized the house to welcome her and make her transition smooth. My uncle led this effort, ensuring everything was in place for her to succeed.

These conversations also touched on the adjustments we would need to make, to accommodate another adult in our living space, regarding privacy and shared responsibilities.

Alain didn't feel comfortable with the change. He feared losing his independence and was always concerned about having Madeline around. His struggle with the existing rules was evident.

Life in Ngok Mapubi continued as usual, but I couldn't shake the feeling that something was quietly changing. Each day, I brought new experiences, leaving me unsure of the shifts happening around me.

Little did I know that the calm in Ngok Mapubi would soon be disrupted, and secrets would start to emerge in ways I could never have imagined.

Reflection

Our time in Ngok Mapubi showed that life is full of twists and turns. What seemed like a peaceful retreat revealed much more. For those of us navigating family life, this experience reminds us that nothing stays the same for long, even in the quietest places. I hope you see the parallels in your life when you thought you had everything figured out, only to realize there was more to discover. Whether it's the relationships that shape us, the environment that influences us, or the secrets that come to light, life keeps us alert. And like in this village, sometimes the unexpected teaches us the most. Every shift, no matter how small, offers a chance for growth. Who knows? The next chapter might be the one that changes everything.

Chapter 6: The Painful Revelation

Ngok Mapubi was a village where life moved slowly, but something was waiting to erupt. At ten and a half, I believed I knew my world, but one day, it would reveal truths that changed everything.

Life there brought both joy and difficulties. The calm of our surroundings contrasted with the undercurrents within our home. One ordinary day, unease grew among us as we went about our tasks. My uncle's new lifestyle left a gap, and the strain between us was evident.

****

Alain continued to be hostile, often directing his anger and frustration toward me. His words were sharp, and his behavior was hurtful. As we played outside one afternoon, he taunted me.

"You're such a loser," he sneered. "Enfant bâtard! Do you know what that means? A child with no father, someone born out of wedlock. A waste of society."

The words cut deep, and tears sprang to my eyes. I always believed that my uncle was my father, both in my mind and heart. He was my dad.

'When Dad returns, I will tell him what you did to me.' Through my tears, I tried to stand my ground, shouting back. Alain's response was swift and harsh. He struck me in the stomach, knocking the wind out of me. I tumbled over, gasping for breath as he ran off, leaving me sobbing on the ground. The pain was intense, but the turmoil overwhelmed me.

Hearing my cries, Pauline rushed over from the house. She knelt beside me, asking what happened. I told her about Alain's words and the hit. Her expression hardened, anger and sorrow flashing across her face. She pulled me close, reassuring me that it would be okay and that we would talk to Uncle when he got home. 'You don't deserve to be treated like this,' she said.

The hours that followed were a blur. Pauline stayed by my side, offering support. Despite her presence, my mind wrestled with thoughts and questions. The idea that my uncle might not indeed be my father was too painful to comprehend. If he wasn't my father, then who was? Why had this been kept from me for so long?

While I was climbing the stairs, Alain was waiting at the top with a cruel grin. He shoved me hard, and I fell to the bottom, landing on my hip. Pain spread through my body, and blood trickled from a cut on my forehead. I could hear Alain laughing, mocking my pain.

I lay there, unable to move, feeling broken. The pain was intense, but the sense of hopelessness was even worse. I felt all alone.

Moments later, Pauline found me. She helped me to my feet and tended to my wounds. 'This has to stop,' she said. 'You can't live like this.'

After another cruel incident, she pulled me aside. 'Don't worry. When Uncle gets home, everything will be okay, and when Madeline moves in, it'll be easier for you.'

Dread settled in my stomach at the thought of facing my uncle. I needed answers, but I was terrified of what they might reveal.

A car pulled up to the house, signaling my uncle's return. My heart raced as he entered, wearing his usual warm smile. Pauline and I exchanged glances, and she gave me a nod. This moment felt different as a defining point in my young life. The man I had always known as Dad now seemed like a stranger. At ten and a half, the news I was about to confront him with was overwhelming.

As he stepped into the room, his smile faded when our eyes met. 'What's wrong?' he asked. I took a deep breath, the words heavy on my tongue. 'Are you my father?' I asked, my voice trembling.

His eyes widened, his expression turning to shock, as if struck by something he hadn't expected. The room held its breath. After a moment, he collected himself, his gaze moving to Pauline. She understood the need for privacy, and quietly left the room. Alain was nowhere in sight, in his room, unaware of the unfolding drama.

The reality of the situation filled the room, making everything feel heavy. The familiarity of our relationship seemed to fade. The revelation had shaken the foundation of my world, and the man I had always called Dad now stood before me, struggling with the same disorientation.

He knelt at my level, and the moment felt like the climax of a scene in a movie, the soundtrack of our lives building in the quiet, intimate space. The truth was about to be revealed, forever changing the story of my childhood.

'Who told you I wasn't your dad?' he asked softly.

'I thought she should know,' Alain said, avoiding direct eye contact. Every word and movement added to the moment.

'This isn't your place, Alain. What you did was wrong and hurtful.' Alain's expression changed, showing a flicker of remorse. 'I'm sorry,' he said, but the apology felt empty, given the harm he had caused. His actions had shattered our family's peace and trust.

With the door closed behind them, I stood in the middle of the room, trying to understand what had just happened. The man I had always known as my father, was actually my uncle. What did that mean for me, for us? My heart ached with the weight of this revelation, and I felt lost.

I loved him deeply, which hadn't changed, but now I wasn't sure how to address him. Dad and uncle felt different in a way I couldn't yet understand. What had been simple was now complicated by a truth I was still trying to process.

I felt betrayed, not because he had deceived me, but because my world had been turned upside down, without warning. My place in the family was now unclear, filled with questions and doubt. I tried to hold onto the past, but everything felt different now.

There was also a flicker of anger directed at Alain, for shattering the innocence of my understanding. Why had he felt the need to tell me? What did he gain from it? His actions felt like a betrayal, leaving a scar on my heart that I wasn't sure would ever heal. I still felt a deep love for the man who had raised me. He had been my protector, my guide, my everything. The titles didn't matter—he was still the man who had nurtured and cared for me.

But the questions remained, always lingering in my thoughts. How would our relationship change? Would things be different between us?

I wanted to cry, scream, and make sense of it all. But no matter what, I knew my feelings for him wouldn't change. Whether I called him Dad or Uncle, he was still the person who had been there for me. I held onto that love, hoping it would guide me through this turbulent time. I needed his support more than ever.

Change was never easy, but it was a necessary part of growth. Looking at my uncle, my dad, and the family we were becoming, I knew we would face whatever came our way together. I adjusted to the new dynamic. It wasn't about titles or bloodlines but the bond we shared. With this in mind, I was ready to move forward.

Reflection

The news that my uncle, whom I believed was my father, was not actually my dad, turned my world upside down. I felt betrayed and lost. My relationship with my uncle, now clearly defined as my father, remains vital to me.

Adjusting to Madeline's presence and the new family dynamics was part of our growth. We faced this change together, supported by the love we share. This experience taught me that family is about the bonds we build, not just names or connections. I'm ready to move forward with this in mind.

Chapter 7: A New Beginning and Unforeseen Tensions

Moving days were supposed to be exciting, but they often came with chaos in our house. Boxes were stacked in the hallways, and the kitchen was full of clashing opinions. The scent of fresh paint hung in the air. When Madeline arrived, she faced a new home and a storm of family dynamics.

****

Moving days were supposed to be exciting, but they often came with chaos in our house. Boxes were stacked in the hallways, and the kitchen was full of clashing opinions. The scent of paint hung in the air. When Madeline arrived, she faced a new home and a storm of family dynamics.

On the day Madeline moved in, the house was busy with activity. Boxes were everywhere, and the paint smell was strong from recent touchups my uncle had insisted on. Madeline, always composed, directed the movers, with her soft voice carrying over the noise.

"Can you help me with this?" she asked, handing Alain a box labeled "kitchen." He had been reticent since the announcement of her moving in, and took the box without a word. I noticed his jaw tighten as he carried it away. He wasn't happy about the situation, so he avoided her and kept his distance.

Madeline noticed Alain's reaction, too. She saw him walk away, understanding that winning him over wouldn't be easy, but was willing to try.

When the last box was carried in, Madeline smiled and thanked everyone. "This is going to be a new chapter, for all of us."

My uncle put an arm around her shoulder and said, "We're all glad you're here, Madeline."

That night, we had dinner together, the first of many. We celebrated our new living arrangement, but Alain remained distant, offering only curt responses and showing his discontent.

After dinner, I overheard my uncle speaking softly to Madeline. "Take your time," he said, "but I know they'll come around, especially Alain."

Madeline leaned into him. "I hope so. I want this to work not just for us but for the kids, too."

My uncle nodded, deep in thought.

Madeline soon brought the order to our home. Breakfast became a family affair, with everyone gathering around the table. The smell of fresh coffee and the sight of scrambled eggs and toasted bread became a regular start to our day.

"Alain, can you pass the jam?" Pauline asked one morning, her voice light and cheerful.

Alain handed it over, but Madeline caught his slight eye roll. She said nothing but smiled briefly before asking with her usual grace.

School days were followed by evenings together. Madeline's steady presence brought us closer.

Alain, however, resisted. He argued with her over minor issues, like dinner times and kitchen organization. After a particularly petty argument, my uncle had enough. He stood up and said, "This behavior has to stop. Madeline is part of this family now, and you must respect that."

Alain's defiance was apparent, but my uncle's tone made him back down. He stormed off to his room, leaving the rest of us in silence.

Madeline, looking down, said quietly, "I'm not here to take anyone's place. I want to help."

My uncle put his hand on hers. "He needs time," he said. There was a shadow in her eyes, a trace of doubt that she quickly hid.

Alain's behavior improved slightly, though his uncertainty lingered. There were moments when I'd catch him watching her, his expression unreadable, as if he were trying to figure her out but wasn't ready to let his guard down. Something had changed.

As we finished dinner, she started clearing the table. Alain got up to help the first time he had done so. There was a silence as they worked side by side at the sink. Then Alain spoke.

"I'm sorry," he said, struggling with a plate.

She looked at him with surprise and relief. "Thank you, Alain," she said softly. "I know this has been hard on you. It's been an adjustment for all of us."

For the first time since she moved in, Alain looked at her. "I guess I just want things to change."

She responded gently. "Change isn't easy, but it can bring good things. We have to give it a chance."

From that evening on, things began to improve. Behavior became better, and the house slowly returned to normalcy. There were still moments of friction, but they became less. Her presence helped bring a new balance to our home.

As we gathered for dinner, she and my uncle exchanged glances, a silent communication that didn't go unnoticed. After the plates were cleared and dessert was served, she cleared her throat.

"I have Something I'd like to share with you all," she began. I'm pregnant."

The room fell silent. Alain's eyes widened, and a smile touched the corners of his lips.

"Congratulations!" I said, the words escaping before I could stop them.

My uncle's eyes shone with pride. "We're thrilled. It will be a big change, but we're excited."

We spent the next few days discussing how the baby would change things and planning for the future. She was equally excited, but there was tension in her interactions with my uncle that neither addressed.

When we informed them of the news, the real test came with her parents, Josephine and Mogard.

Her parents arrived for dinner that weekend. We sat down, and Madeline took a deep breath before delivering the news.

"Mama, I'm pregnant."

She gasped, her hand flying to her mouth in surprise, while Mogard's eyes widened. He asked about the due date and preparations.

As the initial excitement wore off, Josephine's expression turned serious. "This is wonderful news, but you're not engaged and living together. What will people think? Our community might react negatively."

Madeline looked at my uncle.

"We've talked about this," my uncle said calmly. "For now, the best thing is for Madeline to move back to your house, until we can make things official."

Josephine agreed. "That might be for the best. We'll support you both."

"Mogard, you're always welcome in our home. We'll figure this out together."

The hope in Madeline's eyes dimmed slightly. There was no anger, just acceptance of what had to be done. This separation might have effects we couldn't foresee.

Reflection

The narrative shows how Madeline adjusts to a new environment while dealing with significant news. Some family members' reactions shift from initial acceptance to concerns about societal expectations and judgments regarding her pregnancy.

Responses vary, with some offering support and others expressing hesitation. This contrast highlights the difficulty of merging new relationships with existing ones.

Madeline accepts these challenges, and the story illustrates adapting to new situations and handling personal and social issues.

Chapter 8: Shadows of Change

In the calm at Madeline's parents' house, the air was filled with new beginnings, a wedding, and a baby on the way. There was a vague feeling, like the sensation of being watched alone. Plans were made, secrets were shared, and everyone sensed something significant was coming, but no one said exactly what.

****

Life at Madeline's parents' house was steady. She returned home and returned to her old room, and her parents ensured she had what she needed. My uncle visited often, bringing news from home but always returning in the evening. There was a noticeable absence without her.

When Madeline was six months pregnant, my uncle arrived with something special. After dinner at her parents' house, he took her hand and led her outside. "Madeline, we've been through so much together. Will you marry me?" he asked, holding out a ring. Tears filled her eyes. "I will marry you," she replied.

They celebrated with a small dinner. Her mother brought out a bottle of wine they had been saving. It was a warm evening, for sharing stories and laughter.

With the proposal out of the way, preparations for the wedding continued. They hoped Madeline would soon leave as a married woman, but as the date approached, unexpected changes arose.

My uncle came home with an update. "I've been assigned to deliver a convoy of treasury money from Yaoundé to Ngok Mapubi. It's a big job, and will require careful planning." He went over to Madeline's house and shared the exact details.

Her face fell. "But that's dangerous," she said.

"I know," he replied, taking her hand, "but it's my job. I'll ensure everything is in place, and return as soon as possible."

She suggested, "Maybe Polin could go with you."

Surprised, he asked, "Polin?"

"Yes," she said. "He knows the road well and is trustworthy. Plus, he's not going alone. He'll have two friends, Bobo and Baba. They're strong and reliable."

After considering it, he agreed, "If Polin and his friends are willing, that sounds like a good plan. We're all in this together," she concluded.

As the mission's date approached, Polin and Baba spent hours preparing and reviewing every detail. Two security guards from government officials, Eli and Futa, experienced veterans over 5 feet tall, were also recruited. Maps were spread out on the dining room table, and plans were carefully reviewed. The gravity of the mission was clear to everyone involved.

As everything was packed, Madeline stood quietly in the doorway that evening. "Are you sure you have everything?" she asked.

After checking, he replied, "We are as ready as we can be."

Madeline stepped into the room, wrapping her arms around herself. "I wish you didn't have to go," she admitted.

He looked up. "I know, but this is something I have to do. It's my responsibility."

The next day, the sky remained overcast, and the air was sharp with cold. My uncle and his team packed the last of their supplies into the vehicle, carefully double-checking everything. Madeline, her family, Pauline, Alain, and I waved goodbye as the car rumbled to life, breaking the stillness. There was no turning back. We watched them disappear and hugged each other for support.

Reflection

In that part, calm quickly shifts to stress with unexpected events. It shows how thorough preparation is crucial, as seen in the detailed planning for the convoy mission. Trust and teamwork are key, highlighted by including reliable people like Polin and his friends. Sharing fears and seeking support is fantastic, as shown when Madeline talks with my uncle. Even with careful planning, some things are beyond control. The focus is on mutual support, with everyone coming together to offer encouragement, demonstrating that standing by each other in tough times can be very reassuring.

Chapter 9: Unraveling Secrets

My uncle called regularly with updates. Each time the phone rang, the house fell silent as everyone waited. The day after they left, the phone rang again. I answered. 'Hello,' I said, keeping my voice steady. 'Hey, it's me,' his voice came through the line.

'We've arrived safely in Yaoundé. Everything is going well,' he said.

'That's good to hear. How is everyone?'

'Everyone is fine,' he replied. 'We'll spend the night here, and head out tomorrow to pick up the cargo. We should be back in Ngok Mapubi by Wednesday.'

'Okay, that sounds good,' I said. 'It's just me, Alain, and Pauline at home, but we're doing well too. How's the trip been?'

'It's been long, but not too bad. They're holding up fine. How's school?'

I hesitated, then told him about all the subjects I'd been working on—math, science, English, and literature. 'I'm studying a lot. I want to make you proud at the ceremony next month. I'm aiming for third or second place.'

I could almost see his smile through the phone. 'That's wonderful. I know you'll do great. I'm already proud of you.'

His words warmed me, yet a strange emptiness crept in just before the call ended. Then he said he had to go—someone was calling on the other line, and he needed to hang up. 'Of course,'

I replied, not wanting to keep him longer. 'I love you.' 'I love you too,' he said, and the line went dead.

I hung up the phone, and the house was still. The conversation played over in my mind, refusing to fade. There was a time when talking to him about school was difficult. It felt natural now, yet something about this felt different.

As the day wore on, I couldn't shake the feeling. The challenge would come when they had to transport the cargo back. I tried to push those thoughts aside and focus on my study. I shared the news from the call during dinner with Alain and Pauline. There was relief, but worry remained unspoken.

'He said he'd be back by Wednesday,' I repeated, trying to reassure myself. 'Everything is going according to plan.' Alain's usual spark seemed absent. Pauline offered a small smile, but it felt more like a mask than comfort.

We ate. The usual chatter was gone. The house felt different. We all went to bed.

The next day, Pauline and Alain prepared breakfast and tidied up. Thinking of him influenced their usual morning tasks. Every moment, he hoped that today, he would return. We shared our eagerness, trying to keep busy to avoid doubts.

We planned a special breakfast for him—pancakes with coffee, his favorite. But as time passed and the house filled with the smell of coffee and pastries, the clock ticked on, each minute feeling more extended than the last. As time passed without his arrival, our early optimism slowly turned to worry.

Bedtime arrived again, now replaced by a strange sensation. His absence, usually punctual, raised many questions.

We kept busy by talking, singing, and playing together. As the night deepened, we realized he wasn't coming. We went to bed imagining him walking through the door, ready to share stories from his journey. But as the hours passed, he still didn't return.

The next day, worry settled in like an unwelcome guest. He had been missing for four days, but it didn't seem to bother Madeleine as much as it did us. Her calmness and insistence that we do not contact anyone only raised more suspicions.

After hanging up with Madeleine, I knew we had to act. I called Pauline and Alain for a family meeting in our living room.

'I think we need to call the police. Something isn't right. We can't just sit here waiting.'

Pauline agreed. 'We need to find out what's going on, but we shouldn't tell Madeleine. She would have done it if she wanted us to contact anyone.'

Alain, usually the one to lighten the mood, was silent momentarily before speaking up. 'Let's do it. We can't wait any longer.'

We decided together, and I picked up the phone to call the police.

Later that day, a tall and imposing police officer named Phillip came to our home after school. We sat together, and he asked about my uncle. 'How long has he been missing?' Phillip asked. 'Four days,' I replied. And when was the last time you spoke to him?'

I thought back to our last conversation. He called from Yaoundé the day before he was supposed to return. He said everything was fine and he'd be home soon but never showed up. I think he said he'd be home on Wednesday.

Phillip, taking notes, asked, 'Has anyone else been in contact with him since?'

'We called Madeleine, but she hasn't heard from him either,' Pauline added.

Phillip finished his notes and then looked at us. 'I understand this is difficult, but we'll do everything we can to find him. If you think of anything else, no matter how small, please get in touch with us immediately.'

We agreed, and then he left.

That night, Phillip visited Madeleine's family to ask more questions. It seemed normal, but the next day, when Phillip returned, we learned things didn't go smoothly. This time, a detective named Banga was with him, and their questions focused more on Madeleine's relationship with him. The inquiry confused us, and things grew more complicated with every word exchanged.

After our usual evening tasks, we went to bed. When we woke up the following day, we faced a shock that none of us could have anticipated."

Chapter 10: Echoes in the Forest

The trees stood silently, holding secrets as the villagers went about their day, unaware of what lay beyond. Time moved slowly, with the rustle of leaves and bird calls as the only sounds. But that morning, something happened that changed everything.

****

Hours passed before he finally opened his eyes. When he did, the words he spoke sent chills through the room. "Baboulek," he whispered, his voice barely audible. "Head of treasury... ambush... robbed." The officers exchanged looks as the weight of his words sank in. This man, barely clinging to life, was my uncle. But the story he tried to tell made no sense. His words were jumbled, his sentences broken, as if he were piecing together nightmare fragments.

He spoke of an attack by men who appeared out of nowhere and overpowered them. He mentioned a brutal beating, a place where he was left to die while the others were killed. But as he continued, his story kept changing, as if he was reliving the terror over and over in his mind.

"Baboulek," Detective Banga began, "you said you were ambushed and tied to a baobab tree."

"But that's not all—you mentioned something else," the detective pressed.

My uncle stared at them, unfocused, struggling to recall the previous night. His hands trembled as he spoke again, his voice a low murmur, barely audible to the detectives. "I remember Polin," he said, the name like a curse. "He struck me here." He gingerly touched the back of his head, wincing at the memory. "When I woke up, it was dark. I was alone. The cargo was gone. They took everything—$85,000, gone."

The detectives listened intently, knowing they were piecing together a harrowing story. Early that morning, two hunters had stumbled upon my uncle in the forest—tied to a tree, broken and barely alive. His skin was pale and covered in grime, dirt, and dried blood. His clothes were torn and filthy as if he had been dragged through the mud. The hunters immediately contacted the authorities.

When the authorities arrived at the scene, they found my uncle barely conscious, struggling to breathe. They quickly untied him and assessed his condition. Without identification or any way to communicate who he was or what had happened, they rushed him to the nearest hospital.

At the hospital, doctors worked tirelessly to save him. Hours passed before he finally regained enough strength to speak, and his words were confusing when he did.

The words hung in the room like stones, heavier than the loss of the cargo—a fortune gone without a trace, leaving only my uncle and his shattered memories. Detective Banga's expression hardened. "Polin hit you," he repeated, his voice controlled. "You said your companion turned on you. Why would he do that?"

My uncle's eyes darted around the room, his breath quickening as if he were reliving the fear. "I don't know. I don't know why. It all happened so fast. We were on the road, and then everything went wrong."

Detective Banga pressed on. "And when you woke up, you were in the forest, alone?"

My uncle spoke slowly. "Alone, no sign of Polin, no sign of the others—just me, the tree, and the blood."

His voice trailed off, cracking beneath the weight of the memory. The detective's eyes narrowed, searching for any sign of lies. The story had inconsistencies, but there was a truth in it—a man struggling to understand a terrible experience.

"Baboulek," Detective Banga said quietly, "I need you to focus. We need to know exactly what happened. Every detail matters. Think carefully—was there anything else, anything at all?"

My uncle swallowed hard, his fingers gripping the edge of the bed. "I don't know. It's all a blur. I remember the tree, the pain, the darkness—then nothing. I was just there."

The detectives stayed silent for a long moment, their eyes never leaving my uncle. The room felt tighter, the weight of the situation pressing down on him.

Finally, Detective Banga stood up, signaling the end of the questioning. "We'll speak again," he said, "and we'll find out the truth."

As they turned to leave, the tension temped slightly. My uncle slumped back against the pillow, his eyes closing. The effort to remember had drained what little strength he had left.

We went to the hospital and found my uncle. A wave of relief washed over us as we hugged him—grateful he was alive. He stayed in the hospital for a few days, and the next week, we brought him home. A nurse continued to care for his wounds.

At home, life continued as usual. We focused on our tasks—schoolwork, chores, and meals—while we waited for my uncle to fully recover.

Madeleine and her family arrived not long after. They stayed in the house for the next few weeks, offering help where they could. They cooked meals, cleaned up, and tried to make things as easy as possible for my uncle. But even with their efforts, something was unspoken among us. It was as if we were all pretending things were fine, even though we knew they weren't.

My uncle didn't talk much about what had happened. He spent most of his time resting, sitting quietly in his favorite chair, staring out the window at nothing. When we asked him how he was feeling, he would only nod and give us a small, strained smile. He was still hurting, but he wouldn't let us in.

Days turned into weeks, and our routine slowly began to fray. We sensed that something was about to happen but couldn't shake the feeling, no matter how hard we tried to ignore it.

One evening, as we were eating, there was a knock on the door. The sound echoed through the house, and we knew what it meant before anyone answered.

Detective Banga stood at the door. He wasn't alone; Officer Philip was with him. They exchanged a look before stepping inside.

"We need to speak with Baboulek," Detective Banga said. His tone was serious and made me uneasy. This wasn't just another visit.

They looked concerned. Sitting in his chair, my uncle slowly looked up and met the detectives' eyes. His expression was hard to read.

Without a word, he nodded and stood, wincing as he straightened. The room fell silent as he followed the detective and officer into the next room, the door closing behind them.

We were left in silence. I glanced at Pauline and Alain, but none of us spoke. We all sensed that whatever was happening in that room would change everything.

Minutes passed slowly. The voices came through the walls, but we couldn't hear clearly. Our anxiety grew heavier with each moment.

Finally, Detective Banga stepped out. My uncle followed, looking more exhausted than before. He didn't speak as he returned to his chair.

The detectives didn't stay long. They spoke briefly with Madeleine's family before heading out. As they left, Detective Banga looked back at my uncle before walking away.

The silence after their departure was thick. We knew whatever had been discussed was unresolved, and we felt something was coming.

I wanted to ask my uncle what had happened, but I couldn't find the words. We sat in silence as darkness grew closer. It felt like nothing would be the same.

Two weeks passed, and the situation remained unchanged. We went through our days on autopilot, sticking to our routine, but the impact of what had happened was clear. We were waiting for the next event, unsure of when or how.

On a chilly morning, a knock on the door interrupted us as we prepared for school. The sound rang through the house, and we froze.

I opened the door to find Detective Banga and Officer Philip standing there again. Their faces were calm, but something in their eyes made my stomach tighten. They greeted us quietly.

"We're sorry to disturb you so early," Detective Banga said, looking at my uncle. "We need you to come with us to the station."

My uncle's expression tightened. "What for?" he asked, his voice edged.

Officer Philip stepped forward. "We have some potential suspects related to what happened. We'd like you to look at some photographs and see if you recognize anyone."

I saw my uncle's jaw clench. He agreed without protest, knowing there was no point in refusing.

As we prepared for school, I heard the detective and officer talking quietly. I felt heavy, like something was about to break.

"Are you ready?" Detective Banga asked.

My uncle stood, though hesitation lingered before he moved. He shuffled toward the door, the burden of the past weeks visible in each step. As he followed the detective and officer out, I watched him go, feeling a sinking in my chest. The man who had once seemed unshakable now appeared burdened.

At the station, the detectives tried to make my uncle comfortable. They guided him to a seat in a small, quiet area, offering him a bottle of water as they began with casual conversation. According to the stories, my grandmother told me later, they made an effort to put my uncle at ease before discussing the matter at hand.

"We've heard a lot about you, Baboulek," Officer Philip began. "Your work for the community is admirable."

Detective Banga agreed. "It's not every day we meet someone who's made a positive impact. The people here respect you."

My uncle, surprised by the praise, put on a small smile. He took a sip of water, and space seemed less threatening.

The conversation drifted between his contributions to the community, past achievements, and local events. My uncle engaged with them, sharing anecdotes and memories.

But as the conversation continued, Detective Banga began to steer it toward the reason for the visit. "It's clear you care about this place," he said, now serious. "That's why we need your help. We hope you can help us identify the individuals involved in what happened."

My uncle's posture tensed once more. His gaze lingered on the photograph album, the earlier discomfort returning. "Of course," he replied. "I'll do what I can."

They brought out a photograph album and laid it on the table. "Take your time," Officer Philip said. "Anything you recognize could help."

My uncle leaned forward, his eyes scanning the images. Then, he paused. His hand, moving through the photos, stopped suddenly. He stared at one picture, unable to move.

The face in the photo was familiar. It was someone he had known for months, shared meals with, and stood by him during his recovery. The realization hit him hard.

"Do you recognize her?" Detective Banga asked, his voice now sharp.

My uncle's throat tightened. "Yes," he managed to say. "It's Madeleine."

The silence that followed was suffocating. Detective Banga and Officer Philip exchanged a brief, loaded glance. This was not the reaction they had expected, but it changed everything.

"Are you sure, Baboulek?" Detective Banga asked. "Think carefully. This is important."

My uncle looked at the photograph. "I'm sure," he said. "That's her."

The detectives leaned back, the revelation settling over space. The earlier conversation and praise seemed irrelevant now. The face in the photo had shattered whatever remained.

Reflection

Looking back, the difference between my uncle's ordeal and our daily activities is evident. We continued our tasks, trying to avoid facing the full impact of what happened.

My uncle's struggle to recall events, coupled with his fear, revealed the depth of his trauma. The detectives' efforts to piece together his fragmented memories revealed his confusion. His physical and emotional state reflected the severity of his experience.

They were supportive, yet the underlying discomfort remained. We attempted to maintain a routine, even though it felt strained. My uncle's silence and moments of stillness indicated his effort to cope.

As time went on, it became clear that the situation remained unresolved. The feeling of something impending was strong, and our attempts to keep things steady felt increasingly tenuous. This period highlighted the challenge of handling trauma and maintaining balance.

Chapter 11: Unraveling Truths

The days after the station visit were marked by silence. My uncle, though present, seemed distant, lost in unspoken thoughts. The photograph of Madeleine's brother served as a reminder of the scrutiny now shadowing our lives.

Everything changed when she returned. She must have sensed something was wrong even before the detectives arrived.

****

Detective Banga and Officer Philip came early one morning, bringing with them a new wave of anxiety. My uncle watched them approach, his expression unreadable.

Madeleine was in the kitchen when they entered, moving slowly, as if anticipating the inevitable. The detectives approached her calmly, their voices were steady, but firm.

"We need to talk," Detective Banga said, wasting no time.

She turned to face them, her voice steady yet strained. "What is this about?"

"You know," Officer Philip replied. "We showed Baboulek a photograph, and he identified your brother. We need to understand how his picture ended up in that lineup."

The room seemed to close in. Madeleine's composure faltered for a moment, but she quickly regained control. "I don't know what you're implying," she responded, her voice firm. "Why would he have anything to do with this?"

Detective Banga stepped closer. "That's what we intend to find out. Baboulek recognized him, and now we need answers."

She hesitated, her gaze flickering between the detectives and my uncle, who stood silently in the doorway. After a long pause, she spoke, her voice low and deliberate.

"Yes, that's him in the photograph," she admitted. "But you've got it wrong. I'm not the one you should be questioning. It's Baboulek." She pointed at my uncle.

The accusation landed heavily. His eyes widened in shock as the room grew colder with each passing second.

"What are you saying?" Detective Banga asked.

"He was the mastermind," she continued. "He masterminded everything. He hired my brother and his friends to help him get the money. They were supposed to stage an ambush, make it look convincing, and then vanish with the cash. That's why I was following them—I knew something was wrong, but I didn't realize how deep it went until it was too late."

My uncle took a step back, his face drained of color. "That's not true," he stammered. "I'm the victim here!"

"Enough!" Officer Philip's voice sliced through the chaos. He turned to Madeleine. "Why are you only revealing this now?"

"I was scared. I didn't know who to trust. But now I see that I have to tell the truth. He's the one who orchestrated it all."

Detective Banga turned to my uncle. "Baboulek, you've heard the accusation. What do you have to say?"

He looked at her, betrayal etched on his face. "I didn't do this," he finally managed. "I would never do this."

But then something shifted in him. His eyes hardened, and shock morphed into anger. "You want to talk about who's really behind this?" he spat. "It's her! Her need for more is always pushing for more—she is the reason this happened. She brought her brother and those men into this. She is the mastermind, not me!"

The room crackled with tension as accusations flew. Her face drained of color as my uncle continued, his words fueled by anger.

"She knew exactly what she was doing," he said, his voice shaking. "She set this up, and now she's trying to pin it on me to save herself."

The detectives exchanged a glance, their faces unreadable as they processed the explosive claims. The situation had spiraled out of control, and neither side showed any sign of backing down.

"Enough," Detective Banga said firmly. "We need to get to the truth, and the only way to do that is to bring both of you in for further questioning."

They stood frozen, their eyes locked in a silent battle of wills. The room felt suffocating, the weight of the accusations pressing down on everyone.

As the detectives led them out of the house, I stood in the empty room, my thoughts spinning with confusion. Everything

I thought I knew had been turned upside down. The man who had been like a father to me was now embroiled in a scandal with the woman who had become part of our family.

As the door closed behind them, I was left with one burning question: *Who was telling the truth?*

Reflection

 I stood there, alone in the silence, grappling with the storm that had just passed through our lives. How had things unraveled so quickly? Trust, once the bedrock of our family, had crumbled under the crushing weight of suspicion and betrayal. I had always looked up to my uncle, seeing him as a figure of integrity. Madeleine brought warmth into our home, making us believe in new beginnings. Now, all that seemed like a distant memory, shattered by the accusations they hurled at each other.

 Who was telling the truth? Was my uncle the mastermind, driven by pressure and greed, or was Madeleine the one who had orchestrated everything, concealing her true nature behind a mask of concern? The more I thought about it, the less certain I became. The lines between right and wrong, truth and lies, had blurred, leaving me in doubt.

 As I tried to make sense of everything, one thing became clear: nothing would ever be the same. The anger and betrayal had torn a rift in our family that might never heal. I didn't know where we would go from here, but I knew the answers wouldn't come quickly. The truth was buried deep, and uncovering it would take more than just questioning. It would require confronting the very foundation of our lives and accepting that, sometimes, the people we think we know best are the ones who can hurt us the most.

Chapter 12: Beyond the Familiar

Every story has a turning point, a moment when the past no longer defines the future. For me, that moment came quietly, without fanfare, but it carried the weight of everything that had led up to it. The days of certainty were behind me, replaced by a future stretching out into the unknown. This was when everything changed, and I had no choice but to keep moving forward, even if I didn't know where the path would lead.

****

My uncle was taken to the police station early, his fate hanging in the balance. At the station, they treated him with respect but with suspicion. They offered him water, mentioned his contributions to the community, and then shifted to the real reason for his visit.

A series of photographs were again laid before him once more. My uncle scanned them, his expression unreadable—until his eyes landed on one that made him pause. It was Madeleine's brother, without a doubt. The room seemed to close in around him.

The detective leaned in. "We need the truth," he said. "Who planned this? Who's really behind it?"

My uncle struggled to respond. "I've told you everything I know. I'm not the mastermind. This wasn't supposed to happen."

Hours passed before they released him—not as a free man, but as someone with doubt hanging over him. Madeleine was also released, and that's when the accusations began. My uncle blamed her for the situation, accusing her of being the mastermind, driven by her insatiable demands. In turn, Madeleine turned the blame on him, claiming he had orchestrated everything, manipulating her brother and his friends to execute the plan.

Though both were released without formal charges, the damage was done. They went to their separate homes, and from that point on, they didn't speak. The silence between them grew during the investigation. Madeleine wasted no time; she quickly filed for sole custody of Dorah. Supported by her parents, she sought to cut ties with my uncle completely, accusing him of being unfit and dangerous.

The accusations, anger, and betrayal had torn our family apart. I didn't know where we would go from here, but I knew the answers wouldn't come easily or quickly. The truth was buried deep, and uncovering it would take more than just questioning. It would mean confronting the very foundation of our lives and accepting that sometimes, the people we trust the most are the ones who can hurt us the deepest.

Eight weeks passed until one day, at school, my principal pulled me out of class. This was the first time something like this had happened. She told me someone was waiting for me by the football field. "I don't know what's going on, but I'm here if you need to talk," she said as we walked. Her voice was calm, but it only heightened my anxiety.

The walk to the field felt long, each step weighed down by dread. When we arrived, I saw my uncle standing on the ground, flanked by the detective, the officer, and two others I didn't recognize. His posture was slumped, his hands secured behind his back.

"Can I speak to my daughter for a moment?" my uncle asked.

The detective hesitated but then relented. "Make it quick."

They removed the handcuffs, and I rushed into his arms. "Papa, what's happening? Are you coming home?"

He hugged me tightly, his voice barely a whisper. "I love you, and I'm so sorry for everything. I'll be back, I promise. Don't believe everything you hear, and stay strong for me, okay?"

Tears welled up in my eyes, but I nodded. "I will, I promise."

He kissed the top of my head before they re-cuffed him and escorted him to the waiting car. I stood there, watching them drive away, feeling like a part of me was being taken with him.

Back in the classroom, I felt lost. The principal placed a gentle hand on my shoulder. "Remember, you're not alone in this," she said before I returned to my seat. But I was too overwhelmed to respond.

At home, the day's events felt overwhelming. I turned to my journal, desperate to make sense of the turmoil, but the emotions overwhelmed me. Tears flowed as I finally let go of the pain I had been holding inside.

In the days that followed, I avoided Pauline and Alain. I didn't want to talk to anyone. The news didn't help—everywhere I turned, there were stories of my uncle's involvement, making me feel more isolated and confused.

The village buzzed with rumors, bringing new versions of my uncle's actions each day. The situation rippled through every corner of our lives.

The news of my uncle's ordeal reached his family. Driven by the situation, his siblings, father, and mother decided to come to Ngok Mapubi. I was excited to know that one of them was my mother, Marthe. I imagined a reunion that might bring answers, but that hope was fleeting.

When they arrived, the house quickly turned chaotic. My uncle's family moved through the rooms, gathering whatever possessions they deemed valuable. There was no conversation, no acknowledgment of the life we had once shared in that house. I watched silently as they took what they wanted and left, one by one. My mother, the last visitor I had hoped to see, did the same. Worse, she didn't even acknowledge me. It was as if I was invisible to her, a stranger in the home where I had once felt safe.

The trial date arrived, and my grandmother was the only one who attended. When she returned, her face was pale, her eyes heavy with sorrow. She sat me down at the kitchen table, her hands trembling as she took mine.

"Your Uncle... he's been sentenced to 13 years," she said, her voice breaking. "He can get out after 8, but... he won't be coming home for a long time."

I stared at her, the words failing to fully sink in. "Thirteen years? But what about us?"

She squeezed my hands tightly. "We'll have to find a way to keep going, but it won't be easy. You need to be strong, okay? For him and yourself."

The faint spark of hope I had was snuffed out.

After the trial, the house emptied. My Aunt Régine, who promised to return in two weeks to get us, returned but only took Alain. Pauline went to her family, leaving me with our neighbors, Fatoumatou and Mohamed. I stayed with them for six months, waiting for Régine to come. When she didn't, they called her, letting her know they were sending me to Yaoundé.

When Régine picked up the phone, her voice seemed distant, as if separated by an invisible wall. "I can't come back right now," she said. "Just put her on the bus, and I'll be at the station."

"Are you sure? She's been waiting for you for months," Mohamed pressed.

"I'm sure," Régine replied. "I'll be there when she arrives. She'll be fine."

They put me in a car headed to the city, where I would board a bus to Yaoundé. Régine was instructed to pick me up at the bus station when I arrived. As I sat in the back seat, staring out the window, I realized how alone I was. At 12 years old, I was on another path to uncertainty, once again stepping into the unknown.

As the car moved forward, the weight of uncertainty pressed down on me, suffocating every thought. The world outside blurred, yet inside, everything felt sharp. The journey ahead held no promises, only questions that circled endlessly. I wondered what awaited me at the end of the road. Would Régine be there? Would she even recognize me, or had I become just another burden to be passed along?

The landscape changed as we left the familiar behind, the road winding through places I had never seen, places that felt as distant as the life I once knew. I sat silently, each mile amplifying the feeling that something irreplaceable had been lost forever.

Soon, the city would rise before me, vast and overwhelming. Yaoundé, a place I had only heard of but never truly known, would now be my destination. What lay ahead was uncertain, but I knew there was no turning back.

With every turn of the wheel, I drew closer to a new chapter I had no choice but to face. Whatever awaited me there, I would meet it head-on because that's all I could do. And as the car carried me forward, I realized this was more than a trip to a city. It was a step into a future that was no longer mine.

Reflection

Life as I knew it was over. The bonds that once held our family together had unraveled, leaving us to confront an uncertain future. The accusations and betrayals had left wounds too deep for time alone to heal. I realized then that the answers I sought wouldn't come quickly, and the path ahead would be long and difficult. I would have to confront painful truths and accept that the very people I had depended on might be the ones to break me. Moving forward meant embracing the unknown, with no guarantees of closure or peace, only the relentless passage of time and the hope of finding my way amidst the chaos.

Chapter 13: Hours of Uncertainty

The days leading up to my escape had passed in a blur of pain and fear, each one heavier than the last. Yet, in my mind, a quiet voice whispered something was about to break.

****

At just 12 years old, I was alone among strangers, starting what felt like the most daunting experience. The bus wound through the countryside, and the scenery blurred as we moved farther from what had been my home. Each mile increased my anxiety, deepening my concern about what awaited me in Yaoundé.

The hours dragged on. Hunger gnawed at me, and thirst became a constant companion as the bus jolted over rough roads. The cramped space and long duration tested my patience. Each stop offered a brief escape from the confinement. More passengers boarded, crowding the space further, while others left, heading to their destinations.

As I sat there, my thoughts raced. Would my aunt be there? What if she wasn't? The possibility of reuniting with family, the hope of familiar faces, was the only light in an otherwise daunting experience.

When dusk arrived, the bus reached the station in Yaoundé. The city was a world apart from the quiet streets of Ngok Mapubi—louder, busier, and overwhelming. I stepped off the bus, clutching my small bag, and scanned the crowd for any sign of my aunt.

The station was chaotic, with people moving in every direction, each focused on their journey. I stood there, searching for the familiar face I needed to see. The fear of being left alone in this vast place grew as the minutes passed. I spotted her through the crowd—relief washed over me. The journey's tension eased as I realized I wasn't alone.

We caught a taxi, but she remained distant, not asking how I was. I focused on seeing Alain again. My small brown bag—a backpack with what little I had left—sat beside me. Most of my belongings had disappeared, taken when the family gathered their things in Ngok Mapubi after my uncle's sentencing.

Her house was a modest brick structure on a hill with three bedrooms and two bathrooms. The neighborhood consisted of similar houses, differentiated by their windows—some painted, others fortified with barricades.

Inside, I met the family who would shape my days in Yaoundé. Komo, her husband, was short, light-skinned, and quiet. Patou, one of the 15-year-old twins, had become a handsome teen with a calm demeanor. His twin, Mame, was petite and lively, her energy evident.

The second set of twins, Papi and Mami, were nine. Papi shared Patou's strong appearance and was outgoing, while Mami was quieter and preferred to observe the world from the background.

Then there was Bobby, 12 years old, a bit taller than me, lively, and full of talk. Syntyche, the youngest at six, was petite and quiet, often watching everything around her with wide eyes.

My grandmother, petite and graceful, with calm and wise hazel eyes, was a portrait of strength despite everything.

These people I would now live with each contributing to this new phase of my life.

Inside, the house felt darker than I expected. The living room light struggled to brighten the space, and the small windows let in little daylight. Black curtains blocked what little light could seep in. The furniture was sparse—a small sofa, three chairs, and a dining table for eight. The kitchen was cluttered, with pots and pans scattered about. It wasn't the orderly home I had known. Back in Ngok Mapubi, housekeepers ensured everything was in its place. Here, neglect was evident.

Each bedroom had a simple bamboo bed with a metal spring mattress. My aunt's room was slightly more modern, with a wooden bed and a regular mattress. A Moroccan carpet added a touch of warmth to the room, a small comfort in a place that felt so unwelcoming. I was to sleep in the third room with the girls—Mame, Mami, and Syntyche. They slept on the bed. I was given a hard, traditional, flat bamboo mat on the floor.

My aunt wasted no time explaining the rules. I wasn't to eat at the dining table. My meals would be outside after everyone had finished. I was to clear the table, wash the dishes, clean the house, cook, and serve the family. I would wait until they were done before I could eat. Bedtime came only after all the chores were complete. Playing with my cousins' toys or trying on their clothes was forbidden. My role was to serve, not to belong.

Her response was cold when I asked why she didn't hire someone for these tasks, as my father, Baboulek, had done. Her eyes narrowed as she leaned in close.

"Baboulek, your father? He's not your father. He's your uncle. You're a child no one wants. Think about it—your mother and father left you, and the man you call father is in prison for 13 years. You're here because no one else will take you. This is my house, and you'll follow my rules. At least you have a place to stay."

Her words cut deep. I wasn't just unwanted; I was a burden. From that moment, I never questioned her again. I understood my place: a servant in my family with no escape. What made it worse was knowing that my grandmother, who lived under the same roof, was unaware of my situation. My aunt made it clear that if I ever told her, there would be severe consequences.

My life became a routine of endless tasks and relentless labor. Day after day, I was at the mercy of my aunt's temper. A single mistake—a pot placed in the wrong spot, a floor not cleaned to her satisfaction, or a delay in washing her family's clothes in the river—could result in a beating. I washed by hand, ironed everything until it was crisp, and presented it to her, hoping that today, perhaps, I had done enough.

She made it clear that school was not an option for me. "You'll never amount to anything," she said, dismissing the idea of learning or growing. So, while her children and Alain went to school, I stayed behind, trapped in a cycle of servitude. This painful existence continued for more than a year, leaving me, at thirteen, deeply immersed in a life that felt more like slavery than anything else.

Over time, I learned to anticipate her moods. If she came home from visiting friends and her eyes narrowed in my direction, I knew to tread carefully. On those days, any slight misstep could result in punishment. If she passed by without a glance, I knew she was in a good mood, and I might avoid her wrath. But those days were rare. Often, I found myself on the receiving end of her anger.

My grandmother gave me a journal for my thirteenth birthday. It became my only refuge. I hid it beneath the bamboo bed, writing in it whenever my aunt was away. It was my escape, the only place to express my thoughts and feelings without fear of discovery. I guarded it closely, knowing the consequences if she found it.

The beatings became a regular part of my life, happening at least ten times a week. After a while, I lost count. But three moments stand out—times when her anger escalated beyond the usual punishments. On those occasions, anything within her reach became a weapon—a stool, a chair, even a machete. She slammed me against walls, her fury knowing no bounds.

One evening, I was responsible for cooking dinner for the family. I made a traditional meal—Bifaga with combo sauce and fufu. Bifaga is a well-known local fish, often dried and preserved, known for its pungent flavor. The combo sauce, a blend of various ingredients, including tomatoes, onions, and spices, is designed to enhance the fish's richness. Fufu, a staple in many West African households, is a dough-like consistency made from fermented cassava or yams, usually served alongside soups or stews.

Determined to get the seasoning right, I carefully stirred the sauce, letting the flavors blend. The aroma filled the kitchen as the Bifaga absorbed the spices. As the dish simmered, I took a spoonful to taste. The sauce was hot, so I blew on it before cautiously bringing it to my lips, unaware that my aunt was watching.

Suddenly, I felt her hand grip my hair tightly. Before I could react, she slammed me against the concrete wall of the kitchen. Pain shot through my head, and for a moment, I saw stars. This was the first time she hit me with such force. The sudden violence left me stunned and fearful of what would come next.

On another occasion, I went to the nearby river to wash everyone's clothes. It rained heavily that day, and the river water turned murky with mud. When I returned home, my Uncle Komo's white shirt wasn't as white as my aunt expected. I tried to explain the condition of the river, but this only enraged her. She began shouting at me, her voice rising with each insult. She called me a loser and blamed me for her miseries, accusing me of consuming most of the food and expressing her frustration with me.

Her anger escalated, and she grabbed a chair, striking me with it. When that didn't satisfy her, she reached for a machete. Fear gripped me, and I ran, seeking refuge in the girls' room—a big mistake. She followed, banging on the door with the machete, demanding that I come out. When I finally did, she used the flat side of the machete to beat me.

The pain was excruciating. She left me bleeding and sore for days. Despite the constant abuse, I held on to a small hope that someday things would change. I dreamed of freedom, of running far away and never coming back. I prayed for a miracle that might offer a better life.

My Uncle Baboulek was now serving his sentence at Kondengui, the central prison in Yaoundé, Cameroon. Kondengui is infamous in the region for its overcrowded, harsh conditions. Located in the heart of the city, it houses thousands of inmates, many enduring long sentences under extreme heat, inadequate food, and limited access to necessities. Despite the grueling environment, my uncle was granted one day every quarter to leave the prison in the morning and return by evening—a fleeting taste of freedom in an otherwise grim existence.

His first visit came two weeks after the second incident with my aunt. When he arrived at my aunt's house, the atmosphere shifted. There was a rare warmth and excitement as the family gathered around him. They spent hours talking, reconnecting, and momentarily forgetting the heavy reality of his situation. But by the afternoon, my uncle noticed my absence. He asked where I was, and they told him I wasn't there. My uncle was persistent. He insisted on seeing me, and eventually, Alain was sent to find me.

Alain found me outside, playing alone as usual. I had learned to keep to myself, creating little worlds out of the grass, pretending they were dolls—my only companions in this place where I was more a burden than a person. Alain told me I was needed inside, a request that felt foreign and unsettling. I was rarely allowed to be part of their company.

When I entered the room, my uncle greeted me with a warm, familiar hug. His eyes quickly scanned me, noticing how much weight I had lost. Concern clouded his face as he asked if I was eating well. Before I could answer, I felt my aunt's eyes bore into me, her gaze icy and threatening. I knew I had to lie. "Yes, I'm eating well," I told him, forcing a smile. He then asked if my aunt was taking good care of me. I lied again, saying she was a good Aunt and that life was exemplary.

But my uncle's eyes told me he didn't believe me. There was sadness, a concern he couldn't express fully at that moment. As he prepared to leave, he asked me to walk with him. I agreed. We walked together, and I felt the chill of my aunt's anger behind me, her silent wrath a constant threat. It was terrifying, knowing that if I hinted at the truth, the consequences would be severe.

Unable to hold it in any longer, tears welled up in my eyes, and before I knew it, I was crying uncontrollably. My uncle stopped and turned to me, concern etched on his face.

Through my sobs, I begged him to take me with him. "Please, Uncle, take me with you," I cried. "She's the devil. She hurts me, and I'm not in school. I can't do this anymore." The words tumbled out in a rush, years of pain and fear spilling over as I told him everything. I told him about the beatings, the constant work, how I wasn't allowed to go to school, and how I was treated like I didn't matter.

My uncle listened, his expression shifting from concern to shock and anger as I poured out the truth. His grip on my hand tightened as if he was trying to hold onto his own emotions. He knelt to my level, his voice trembling.

"Why didn't you tell me sooner?" he asked, his voice thick with emotion. But I didn't have an answer. The fear of my aunt's retribution had kept me silent for so long.

The weight of my confession was heavy. I spoke the truth but didn't know what would come next. My uncle looked back at the house, his jaw clenched, and then back at me, his eyes filled with sorrow and determination.

"I'm so sorry," he whispered, pulling me into a tight hug. "I'll find a way to make this right."

When he released me, the reality of our situation hit hard. My uncle was still a prisoner, bound by his chains at Kondengui. But at that moment, I felt a small glimmer of hope. For the first time in a long time, someone knew the truth. Someone cared.

After I told my uncle everything, he held me close, his voice steady but filled with sorrow. "You need to go back," he said softly. "Obey her and try your best to do everything even better. Strive for perfection, even if it feels impossible."

His words cut through the pain, and though I wanted to leave with him, I knew I had no choice. His sentence bound him, and I was still under my aunt's control. But his advice stayed with me, and when I returned home, I resolved to do just as he said. I worked harder, longer, and with more determination, pushing myself to go beyond what was asked of me. I learned to anticipate my aunt's demands and tried to stay ahead of her expectations.

There was a noticeable change when my uncle returned for his next visit three months later. This time, he didn't just come to see the family—he came to act. He took me to a local high school and enrolled me himself. Standing in the school's office, I felt a mix of disbelief and relief. For the first time in a long while, it felt like things might change.

My uncle spoke to my aunt afterward, clarifying that I was to attend school regularly. He promised to send her a small allowance from his limited prison pay to cover my expenses and ensure I had what I needed for school. He emphasized that my education was a priority and expected her to support it.

With my uncle's support, I continued to excel in my responsibilities at home and my studies at school. The school routine brought a new sense of purpose to my life, a small but significant escape from the harsh reality of my home life. Although the beatings didn't stop entirely, they slowed down, and the fear that had once consumed me began to ease, if only slightly.

Until the day I let my guard down. After completing my homework, my aunt asked me to cook her favorite dish: silure, a type of black fish in Cameroon. It's often prepared as Bongo Chobi, a dark, aromatic sauce made from burnt spices, typically served with Bobolo, a fermented cassava stick wrapped in leaves. Combining the tender, smoky fish with the dense, tangy Bobolo is a dish that carries tradition and weight—a meal that demands precision.

Determined to do everything perfectly, I focused on each step. The fish simmered in the pot, its aroma filling the kitchen with the promise of a proper meal. I stepped away to grab the final ingredients, unaware of the silent shadow that moved behind me. Everything was in place when I returned—until dinner was served.

My aunt stormed into the kitchen, her face a mask of rage. She accused me of stealing the food, her voice sharp and cold. Before I could process her words, she spat in my face, a sudden, shocking act that left me frozen. Her hand shot out, gripping my neck with such force that the world around me blurred. I felt her fury in every inch of her grip, as if she wanted to crush the life out of me. After another round of blows, she dragged me outside.

In the dim light of the yard stood the rusty metal cage where she kept her dogs. Without a word, she shoved me inside, locking the door with a final, ominous click. The cage was cold, the metal bars pressing into my skin. I could feel the dogs' presence, their eyes glowing in the dark, their growls low and threatening. That's where I spent the night, huddled in a corner, terrified and alone.

As the night stretched on, each second was an eternity. A soft rustling caught my attention. Mana Ndongo, the neighbor, had seen everything. She approached cautiously, slipping some food through the bars. But the dogs were restless, their growls turning to snarls as they snapped up most of it before I could get more than a few bites. Hunger gnawed at me, but worse was the overwhelming sense of dread that seeped into my bones.

When morning came, my aunt unlocked the cage, her face unreadable. I didn't wait for an explanation—I ran straight to my grandmother's room. The moment she saw me, she knew. Her eyes filled with pain and fury as she confronted my aunt, demanding the truth. But my aunt's lies were smooth, denying everything. Komo, her husband, stepped into the room, piecing together the situation with a look of cold calculation. His eyes narrowed, and without warning, he turned on me.

A frail but fierce grandmother tried to protect me, stepping between us. But they pushed her aside, her body crumbling to the floor like a rag doll. Fear spiked through me, and I bolted from the house, my heart pounding in my chest. I ran to Mana Ndongo's house, breathless and desperate. She quickly hid me under her bed, whispering reassurances as I lay trembling in the dark.

From my hiding spot, I heard the wail of an ambulance. My heart sank, realizing it must be for my grandmother. Fear and guilt twisted in my gut, but I dared not move. Soon after, Komo's heavy footsteps approached the tiny home. He demanded that Mana Ndongo turn me over, threatening her with chilling calmness. But she stood her ground, insisting I wasn't there, promising to inform him if she found me.

Once he left, Mana Ndongo waited until nightfall. She handed me a blanket, a small bag of chips, a bottle of water, and 5000 CFA. "Go "find somewhere safe. I'll help you as much as I can."

That night, with only a few belongings, I became homeless. My heart raced as I moved, unsure of where I was going or what lay ahead. But one thing was clear—I couldn't go back. Not now, not ever.

I disappeared into the night, a cold grip settling over me. This marked the start of something new and perilous. I didn't know where I was headed or what awaited me, but I knew one thing: I could never return.

Reflection

    Even now, I still feel how my stomach churned on that bus. The fear of the unknown was almost overwhelming, but there was also a strange relief. Have you ever found yourself in a situation where you felt utterly alone, unsure of what the next moment would bring? That was how I felt in those final days—like I was standing on the edge of a cliff, with no idea if I would fall or find a way to fly.

Chapter 14: Lost and Found: The Streets of Yaoundé

This story is about survival and the will to keep going when everything feels like it's falling apart. It represents a turning point—a moment when, despite everything, I realized that hope, determination, and dreams were still within reach.

Thank you for accompanying me on this journey. I hope my story resonates with something profound within you, reminding you of your strength and resilience in the face of life's challenges.

****

The night closed in around me, haunted by fears I had carried for as long as I could remember. The cool air felt sharp against my skin, carrying distant sounds that seemed to echo with an unsettling presence. The fears I was trying to escape pressed in, relentless and unyielding.

Panic surged through me, cold and fierce, and before I knew it, I was running. My feet pounded the ground, each step jarring as if the earth was trying to pull me back. The wind stung my eyes, and the trees blurred into a terrifying mass. My breath came in short, ragged gasps, my thoughts a mix of fear and confusion. I had no idea where I was headed—only that I had to keep moving.

I found myself in a cornfield. The tall stalks surrounded me, their rustling leaves adding to my panic. Each rustle felt like the presence of something menacing, just out of sight. I was lost in a maze, anxiety gnawing at my stomach, making it hard to breathe. But I couldn't stop—I wouldn't stop.

Through the night, I saw a small and distant but steady light. It became my anchor, the one thing that kept me from drowning in fear. I fixed my eyes on it and ran harder, pushing through the corn. Each step brought me closer, the light intensifying, pulling me out of the maze and into a small clearing.

As I reached the clearing, I realized the light wasn't some distant star or far-off hope—it was a lamp hanging over a street vendor's stand. The vendor, an older man with kind eyes, served food to late-night customers. The lamp's warm illumination bathed everything in a soft, golden light, and the world didn't seem so frightening for a moment.

But that comfort faded as the reality of where I was sunk in. I had run from Ékounou to Yaoundé Central—at least five kilometers or more. Landmarks and city sounds rushed back, bringing an understanding of my situation. I was alone. I had no one to turn to, no home to return to. The freedom I had fought for suddenly felt hollow. I was free, but I was also homeless, a child lost in a city that did not care.

The truth was overwhelming. Tears welled up, blurring my vision, and I let them fall. I stood there under the dim light of the streetlamp and cried. The world around me kept moving, indifferent to my pain, but I couldn't hold it back. Fear, exhaustion, and loneliness all poured out with those tears. I cried until there was nothing left, just a deep, aching emptiness.

When the tears finally stopped, I wiped my face and started walking, unsure where to go or what to do next. The city felt foreign. The dumpsters I passed were overflowing, their stench rising in thick waves. It was as if this part of the city had been forgotten, left to rot while the rest of Yaoundé moved on. The contrast was striking—on one side, filth and decay; on the other, the bright lights of the city's towering buildings, symbols of power and wealth. I couldn't understand how these two worlds could coexist.

The streets around me were alive with contradictions. The smell of rot, overflowing dumpsters, stray dogs scavenging for scraps, and the heavy weight of poverty pressed down like a blanket. But just a few steps away, towering buildings gleamed under the city lights, their presence a stark reminder of the wealth and power that seemed so distant. The contrast was jarring, a physical representation of the division I felt within myself—a tug-of-war between despair and hope.

Eventually, after wandering for what felt like hours, I found myself in front of the supermarket SCORE; bright lights stood in stark contrast to the grimy roads surrounding it. The glass windows reflected the city's glow, making the store look like a beacon. It felt safe, or at least safer than where I had been. I decided this would be where I stayed, at least for the night.

I found a piece of cardboard, discarded and worn, and dragged it to a spot near the store. It wasn't much, but it was enough. I cut the cardboard, shaping it into a bed, and then wrapped myself in the blanket Mandongo had given me. The pavement was hard beneath me, but I was used to that. It was no different from the floor at my aunt's house; it was just a new kind of hard. The blanket was my only comfort, a small reminder of the life I had just left behind.

Morning came too quickly, heralded by the clattering of metal shutters. The store was opening, and the workers were arriving, their footsteps on the pavement like a wake-up call I wasn't ready for. I blinked against the early light, gradually realizing where I was. Shame washed over me as I hurried to sit up, pulling the blanket tightly around me as if it could somehow shield me from the world. I felt exposed, vulnerable, and, worst of all, ashamed. I felt like a beggar with nowhere to go.

The noise of the workers and the store's opening brought a rush of thoughts. My first instinct was to run again, to find my way to Kandengi and seek out Uncle Baboulek. Perhaps he would take me in and help me figure out what to do next. But that thought was immediately crushed by reality. Baboulek was in prison, serving a 13-year sentence. There was no help to be found there. I couldn't face him, not that it was even an option. The shame of running away and the fear of being seen as a failure were overwhelming. I couldn't bear admitting that I had nowhere else to go.

My thoughts turned to my grandmother. The last image I had of her was seared into my mind: her frail body slumped against the wall, her head hitting the hard surface with a sickening thud as she tried to shield me from the blows. I remembered the panic in her eyes, the way she fought for me even as they dragged me away. Then the ambulance arrived, and she was gone, taken to the hospital. I couldn't go back there either. The thought of seeing her hurt again, knowing it was because of me, was unbearable.

I was once more completely isolated, and the weight of that truth nearly crushed me. There was no going back, no one to turn to. I had to survive, somehow, on my own.

I scanned the area, desperate to find anything that could help me. The dumpsters behind the food stand caught my eye. They were overflowing with trash, the smell wafting through the air in an intense cloud. It was disgusting, but I didn't care. Somewhere in that mess, there might be something I could eat. I didn't have the luxury of being picky; I was hungry, and hunger dulls the senses. The idea of scavenging for food didn't disgust me—it was necessary to stay alive.

But food wasn't the only thing I needed. I needed to clean up, use a bathroom, and find some semblance of normalcy in this chaotic new reality. I remembered the small movie theater near SCORE. It wasn't much, but it was something that provided what I needed. I made my way there, keeping to the shadows, waiting for the right moment to slip inside unnoticed. The guard was distracted, talking to someone at the entrance, and I seized the opportunity.

Inside, the theater was dimly lit, the faint smell of popcorn lingering in the air. I headed straight for the bathroom, avoiding the mirrors as I passed. I couldn't bear to see my reflection—the hollow eyes, the messy hair, the clothes that clung to my body like a second skin. I didn't want to confront the reality of what I had become. The mirrors mocked me, reflecting a version of myself I didn't recognize, a version I didn't want to accept.

Sometimes, if lucky, I would sneak into one of the theaters and watch part of a movie. It was a brief escape from the harshness of the streets. I would sit in the darkness, trying to lose myself in the flickering images on the screen, picking up bits of popcorn or food left on the floor. It was barely enough to keep me going. After the movie, I would slip back out, blend into the shadows, and return to SCORE.

Days turned into weeks, and I settled into a routine, a fragile rhythm that kept me alive. The local food vendors—Mohamed, Hamed, and Fatima—became my lifeline. They didn't know much about me, but they recognized me, and that was enough. Sometimes, they would call me over, offering me leftovers or letting me finish what a customer had left on their plate. Much of it was just scraps, but it kept the hunger at bay. For about three and a half months, this became my life—a cycle of scavenging, hiding, and surviving.

Those months were also filled with dark thoughts and moments where I didn't know if I could keep going. My aunt's voice was a constant presence in my mind, her cruel words shaping my fears and fueling my despair. I felt like a burden, a child no one wanted. The sting of rejection from those who should have loved me was too much to bear.

There were nights when I thought about ending it all. The idea of escaping from the pain was tempting. But even in those darkest moments, a small part refused to let go. I remembered the light that had guided me through the cornfield, pulling me out of the darkness when I thought I was lost. That light became a symbol of hope, a reminder that even in the darkest times, something was always worth fighting for.

I started to talk back to the words in my head, to the ghost of my aunt who haunted me. I would find a mirror and look at myself. I saw the girl she had tried to break and who had survived. "You're worth it," I would say to my reflection, my voice barely a whisper at first but growing stronger each time. "You're better than this. You can do more."

It wasn't easy. The shadows were always there, ready to drag me back under. But I chose to fight. I decided to believe that I was more than the sum of my past, more than the broken child my aunt had tried to make me. I was a survivor, and with even a smaller chance, I knew I could find a way out.

One night, wandering the empty streets, the city seemed to stretch on endlessly, every corner a reminder of how alone I was. My legs ached from walking, and exhaustion pressed down on me. The streetlights flickered above, casting long, distorted shadows that danced eerily on the pavement. The distant hum of traffic was a constant noise in the background, accentuating the emptiness around me.

I wasn't just tired—I was emotionally spent, teetering on the edge of despair. The reality of my situation was sinking in deeper with every step. The thought of giving up, of letting the shadows swallow me whole, was becoming more challenging to push away. But as I rounded a corner, lost in my thoughts, I collided with a couple.

Startled, I looked up, my heart racing. They stood before me, their faces partially obscured by the dim light. The woman was petite, her features soft and kind, and her eyes reflected a deep compassion. The taller and more imposing man had an air of quiet strength. They looked out of place in this desolate part of the city, their concern for me palpable even in the way they stood.

"What are you doing out here alone?" the woman asked, her voice gentle but tinged with worry. Her tone had a slight tremor as if she feared the answer.

The question cut through me. What was I doing out here? The truth was too raw, too painful to share with strangers. The urge to lie, to protect myself, surged up instinctively. I didn't want to be pitied or see that familiar judgment in their eyes.

"I don't have a family," I whispered, my voice barely audible. "They're all dead."

The man's eyes narrowed, studying me. His expression had no malice, just a quiet skepticism that made me uneasy. "Everyone has a family," he replied softly, his tone gentle yet firm. It was a statement, not a question, and hung between us.

His words sent a jolt of panic through me, triggering a flood of memories I had fought so hard to bury. In an instant, I was back in my aunt's house, her voice ringing in my ears: "You're nothing. You'll never amount to anything." The sting of her words was as sharp as ever, cutting into the fragile shell I had built around myself. I could feel tears threatening to spill over, but I forced them back, refusing to break in front of these strangers.

"My parents are dead," I repeated, my voice more assertive this time, though a tremor remained beneath the surface. I was trying to convince them, but more than that, I was trying to convince myself. The lie felt safer than the truth, less painful to hold onto. But even as I spoke, I saw the doubt in their eyes. They knew I wasn't being honest but didn't press me. They didn't need to. The weight of my own words was suffocating.

The woman reached out, her hand hovering just above my arm as if she wanted to comfort me but wasn't sure how. "What's your name?" she asked, her voice softer now.

"Clarissa," I lied again, the name slipping out with surprising ease. It felt like slipping into a new skin that didn't carry the scars of my past. But as soon as the name left my lips, a pang of guilt twisted in my chest. Who was Clarissa? She was no one, a fabrication, a shield to hide behind. But at that moment, she was safer than being Cara.

The couple exchanged a look, a silent conversation passing between them that I couldn't decipher. There was a tenderness in how they looked at each other, a shared understanding that made me feel like an outsider in my own story.

After a moment, the man spoke, his voice steady and sincere. "We've been thinking… If you don't mind, how about we adopt you?"

The very idea seemed like a dream too fragile to grasp. But there was no mistaking the genuine concern in their eyes that made me want to believe them. For a fleeting moment, I let myself imagine what it would be like to belong to someone, be cared for, and have a place in the world.

"Not at all," I finally replied, my voice barely audible, but there was a strength in those words that surprised even me. The relief that washed over me was almost overwhelming, though it was tinged with lingering guilt for the lies I had told. Still, the thought of being wanted and taken in was a lifeline I couldn't afford to refuse.

From that night on, they became my street parents. Their real names, lost to the fog of memory and the trauma of those days, would forever remain "Okay" in my mind. But their kindness, their willingness to take me in despite the lies I told, left an indelible mark on my heart. They were my lifeline, pulling me back from the depths and giving me a reason to hold on.

Though kind, they were far from traditional parents. Our life together on the streets was shaped by survival, and they wasted no time teaching me the harsh realities of it. They knew that the sight of a child begging could stir compassion in even the hardest of hearts, and they saw an opportunity. It wasn't long before they showed me how to pray, a skill that, despite the shame I felt, became a lifeline during those months.

Each morning, just as the sun was beginning to rise and the city was waking up, they would take me to SCORE. The busy supermarket was the perfect spot with its constant stream of customers. They would place me in front of the entrance with a small, worn bucket. The bucket was old, scratched, and dented from years of use, but it was just the right size for a child like me to hold. I would sit there, the bucket in my lap, while people passed by, their hurried footsteps echoing in my ears.

At first, I didn't know how to ask for money. I was too ashamed, too embarrassed by the idea of begging. The words stuck in my throat, choking me with their weight. But my new guardians were patient. They taught me what to say, how to look up at the passersby with wide, innocent eyes, and how to make myself look small and helpless. It felt wrong, but I learned quickly that this was a matter of survival.

The first time I tried, I could barely speak the words. "Please, can you help me?" My voice quivered, but it was enough. A few coins clinked into the bucket, and though the shame burned in my chest, I knew I had to keep going. With each day that passed, it became easier. I learned to position myself right and catch people's attention without intruding. I became good at it—too good.

People would walk by, some averting their eyes and pretending not to see me, while others would stop, look down at me with pity, and drop a few coins into the bucket. The sound of the coins hitting the bottom was bittersweet—a reminder of both the kindness in the world and the depths to which I had fallen. But I learned to push the shame aside and focus on the small victories each coin represented.

They would watch from a distance, never too far, but far enough to give the impression that I was alone. They knew that people were more likely to give if they thought I had no one else. After a few hours, when the bucket was sufficiently full, they would come back and collect me. We would count the money together; each coin testament offered a slight relief to our shared struggle. The goodwill of strangers was enough for the three of us to get by for another day.

In those three months, I learned more about the harshness of life than I had in all the years before. Though kind in their way, my street parents had their scars, their own stories of loss and survival. They never spoke of their pasts, but when we sat together counting the day's earnings in quiet moments, I could see the weariness in their eyes. They were survivors, just like me.

Days turned into weeks and then months, and the burden of this life began to weigh on me. The shame I had pushed aside started gnawing at my conscience. I wondered if this were all I would ever be—a child begging for scraps, surviving on the pity of strangers. I wanted more, even if I didn't know what that was yet. For now, I had to keep going.

Life on the streets was a constant cycle of survival but had its small moments of joy. My street parents, despite our harsh existence, found these moments. After a long day of begging in front of SCORE, they would play a simple game with rocks. It was a game of speed and precision, bringing us together in a way that nothing else could.

We'd sit in the dirt, laughing as the rocks clattered, mingling with the distant city noise. Those moments made me forget my situation and feel like a child again. I became good at the game, which reminded me that even in bleak circumstances, there was room for play and connection.

But life was unpredictable. One night, after we had gathered coins and played our usual game, my street parents left earlier than usual. They told me to wait for them at our spot, something we had done many times before. This time, they didn't return.

I initially didn't worry. It wasn't unusual for them to be gone for a while. I sat with my bucket, scanning the crowd for any sign of them. As the sun set and the crowd thinned out, they still hadn't returned.

I waited, telling myself they would be back soon. But as night fell and the streetlights came on, I realized something was wrong. Panic began to set in, but I forced it down, hoping they would return.

I went back to SCORE, thinking they might be there. I walked the dimly lit streets, heart heavy with anxiety. When I reached SCORE, I waited again, sitting on the cold pavement, eyes fixed on each passerby. But they never came.

Desperate, I searched the streets, retracing our usual paths. I visited Fatima's stall and passed by vendors we knew, but none had seen them. The city that had once felt familiar now seemed like a maze of loneliness.

Hours passed, and it became clear they weren't coming back. They had left without a word or goodbye. I felt abandoned and discarded, like the rocks we used to play with scattered on the ground.

Doubts resurfaced. My aunt's cruel words echoed: "You're nothing. You'll never amount to anything." Maybe no one wanted me. The questions swirled, cutting deeply. I began to believe I was the problem, destined to be alone.

Wandering through the empty streets, I hoped to find them and understand why they had left. But the city was silent, and the only sound was the echo of my footsteps.

As the night wore on and the city grew quieter, exhaustion set in. The streets that once seemed full of possibility now felt like a maze with no escape. My hope of finding them slipped away.

I retraced my steps back to SCORE. The cold pavement, flickering streetlights, and the distant hum of the city felt different now, tinged with abandonment. I was no longer the child with a worn bucket; I was lost, searching for something never meant to be found.

A deep voice broke the silence as I neared SCORE, the familiar glow of the store's lights. It came from the shadows, rough and gravelly yet almost paternal.

"My child, where are you going this late at night?" the voice asked, its words offering a lifeline and pulling me back.

I froze, my heart pounding, torn between fleeing and facing the darkness. Yet something in the voice made me stop. I wasn't alone for the first time in what felt like an eternity. Someone had seen, spoken to, and called me "my child." The night wasn't over, but something had shifted. And though I didn't know it then, this was the beginning of a new chapter in my time on the streets.

Reflection

Looking back, I see how those dark moments shaped who I am today. The streets taught me resilience and revealed the depth of human kindness—even in the most unexpected places.

Small acts of compassion kept me going when I was lost and scared. The street vendors who shared leftovers, the couple who took me in, and even the strangers who dropped coins into my bucket reminded me that I was seen and mattered.

The most significant lesson I learned was the importance of hope. During those times, hope was like a distant light—it wasn't always bright, but it guided me. It prevented me from giving up, even when everything seemed bleak.

I also discovered the power of self-belief. Facing the negative messages in my head that told me I was worthless marked a turning point. I learned that we could reshape the narratives others impose on us and see ourselves not as victims but survivors with the strength to overcome.

To anyone feeling lost, unwanted, or overwhelmed, remember that your story isn't over. There is always hope, even in the darkest times. You have the strength to keep going, find your way out, and create a life worth living.

Chapter 15: Against the Current

As you enter this chapter, consider the moments when your life stood at a junction. Have there been times when choices appeared out of nowhere, decisions that could change everything? What thoughts crossed your mind when you stood at the edge of the unknown, unsure whether to move forward or hold back? Think about the voices in your life that have guided, comforted, or even haunted you. Have these voices shaped your decisions? Were there times when you ignored them, only to realize later their significance? Or perhaps you followed them, trusting in their guidance, and found yourself on a path you never expected.

Reflect on moments when hope and fear collided. When did you last feel the pull of something greater or a potential calling from uncertainty? What did you do with that feeling? Did you chase it or let it slip away? Think of the relationships in your life, the people who walk beside you, and the strangers who cross your path. Have these encounters shaped who you are today? Have seemingly small meetings led to significant changes?

Let these questions guide you. Explore the unknown and embrace the uncertainty. This chapter is not just about my story—it's an invitation to reflect on your journey.

****

In the silence of the city that never truly sleeps, where the night carried its secrets, and faint lights glowed in the distance, a voice cut through the stillness, sharp and clear: "My child, where are you going at this hour?"

The words stopped me in my tracks. It wasn't just what he said but the warmth behind them—my child. Those words hadn't been spoken to me in years. Slowly, I turned around, my breath catching. There stood a tall figure dressed in a dark suit, entirely out of place in the gritty streets of Yaoundé. His white shirt gleamed under the streetlights, untouched, as if he had stepped out of another world, far removed from the one I knew.

For a moment, I couldn't speak. Was this man my father? Could he be the figure I had never met but always wondered about? Or was he sent by my father's family, someone who had come to find me? I allowed myself, just for a moment, to believe I wasn't as alone as I felt.

"My child," he said again, his voice gentle yet firm, "What are you doing here alone? What's your name?" His question lingered, sending a ripple of fear through me. On the streets, I learned to guard my identity and create personas that protected me from the world. I hesitated before answering, uncertain of who I should be.

Without another word, he guided us toward one of the food stands. The vendor greeted him with a nod, and soon, he had ordered something—soup, bread, maybe some meat. It was more than I could have imagined. The food wasn't just soup or bread, though it smelled good. It felt like something I hadn't experienced in a long time.

The man asked, "Are you hungry?"

"Yes," I replied, the words slipping out before I could stop them. Admitting my hunger felt like a minor defeat, a vulnerability I wasn't used to showing, but the hunger was real, and the food was too tempting to resist.

As I ate, each bite took me back to a different time. Memories of my life in Ngaoundéré with my uncle Baboulek played in my mind. I saw the grand villa, the laughter, the rooms that had once been full of comfort. I remembered the large dining table, my uncle at the head, and the maids serving us with care. That life felt like another world now—one I had lost but never forgotten.

After eating, he looked at me with the same kindness, almost paternal. "Do you need a ride home?" he asked.

The word "home" felt foreign, like a distant memory I could no longer grasp. "I don't know," I said, trying to sound confident, but the uncertainty slipped into my voice. "I'm fine. It's okay."

He didn't push. Instead, he reached into his pocket and pulled out a stack of bills. "25,000 CFA," he said. "That's about 42 dollars."

I stared at the money, trying to understand what had just happened. For someone like me, living on the streets, this wasn't just money—it was hope, a way out. He handed me a small card and said, "Visit me in one of those buildings. That's the Ministry of Finance. Tell the receptionist you met Mr. Bernard and come talk to me."

The name remained with me, and I was unable to respond.

As I watched him go, his figure retreating into the night, my mind reeled. This man, this stranger, had just handed me the money. I clutched it in my hand, almost too much to comprehend. I expected to wake up from some impossible dream.

Slowly, I looked down at the money. My fingers moved over the smooth surface of the bills, the scent of them filling my nose. I counted again 25,000 CFA. It was all there. This money felt like a miracle. It wasn't just paper—it was a chance to escape my life and find my way back to something I had lost.

But then, reality hit me hard. I had told Mr. Bernard that I lived with my grandmother. He asked me to share this story with her and visit him at the Ministry of Finance. My grandmother wasn't in my life anymore. Her home was just a memory I had clung to in moments of fear. The only way I could share this story with her was to return to her. And the thought of going back, of facing the past I had tried to escape, made me hesitate.

The streets had become my reality, and going back meant confronting everything I had left behind—the fear, the failures, the broken pieces of my life I didn't want to face again. But another part of me whispered that maybe Mr. Bernard offered a way out, a chance for redemption. Could I really return to my grandmother and ask for forgiveness?

The thought scared me, but staying on the streets with no future frightened me even more. I knew what I had to do. I had to go back. And so, I did.

With the money still clutched tightly, I turned away from where Mr. Bernard had disappeared into the night. The streets now felt eerily quiet. The journey back felt longer than I remembered, the landmarks blurring together. What would I say to her? How would she react? The questions buzzed in my head. I had to do this.

Approaching the neighborhood where my grandmother lived, my heart raced. The house came into view, its outline in the darkness. The place looked the same, yet different—smaller, more fragile.

I stood at the gate, memories flooding back. The smell of her cooking, the sound of her voice as she prayed over me at night—it had been so long since I had felt any of those things. Standing here, I felt like a child again, lost and seeking safety.

With a deep breath, I pushed the gate open and walked up to the door. My hand hovered over the doorbell for a moment before I pressed it. The sound cut through the stillness of the night. I waited, the seconds stretching out like hours.

I heard someone approaching from the other side of the door. My heart leaped into my throat as the door creaked open, revealing a face I had missed more than I realized.

My grandmother stood there, her face etched with lines of time and worry. She had endured in my absence. Her eyes widened in surprise as she saw me standing on her doorstep, looking worn and weary.

Neither of us spoke, the silence thick with unspoken words.

Finally, she stepped forward. "Cara," she said softly. I couldn't hold back the tears any longer. The dam broke as I rushed into her arms. She held me tight, and I let the tears flow, overwhelmed by the reunion.

But the moment was fleeting. The memories of how my grandmother had been taken away in an ambulance were vivid.

I heard my aunt's voice from the other room. "Who's at the door?"

My grandmother's eyes shifted. "It's her," she called back. "It's Cara."

There was a brief silence, followed by my aunt's sharp voice. "Close the door."

My grandmother hesitated but obeyed, closing the door with a thud. I could hear them talking inside, their voices low but urgent.

My grandmother stepped outside when the door opened again, closing it behind her. "What do you want, Cara?" she asked softly.

I took a deep breath. "I need to talk to you, Grandma," I said. "I need to tell you what happened."

She looked at me with concern. "We can't talk inside," she said. "She doesn't want you in the house."

I wasn't surprised. The memories of how she had treated me, the cruelty, the neglect were still fresh. Once a place of protection, the house had become a reminder of what I had tried to escape.

We stepped away from the door into the cool night air, where we could speak without being overheard. The street was quiet as I prepared to talk.

"I met someone tonight," I began. "A man named Mr. Bernard. He gave me money and asked me to visit him at the Ministry of Finance."

My grandmother's eyes widened in alarm, her face paling. "No, Cara," she said urgently. "You don't know what this man could want from you. He could use you, hurt you. Please, promise me you won't go see him."

Her words stung a fear that pierced through the hope that had begun to take root in my heart. I could see the worry in her eyes, the protective instinct that had always been there. But there was something else, too—a curiosity, a determination, that I couldn't shake. If Mr. Bernard could offer me a way out, a chance at something better, wasn't it worth the risk?

"I'll be careful," I tried to assure her, but I could see it was insufficient. She needed a promise, something definite, something I could not give her.

She reached out, holding me. "Please, Cara," she said urgently. "Promise me."

I hugged her back, feeling the tears prick in my eyes. "I love you, Grandma," I said softly. "But I have to do this."

She did not say anything else; she held me for a long moment. When she finally let go, her eyes were filled with sadness.

"I love you too," she said, her voice breaking.

I turned and walked away. I had made my choice, and there was no turning back.

Tomorrow would come soon enough.

<u>Reflection</u>

I think about the choices I made. The voice that called out to me that night was a moment of significance that changed the course of my life. I wonder if you have ever experienced a moment like that. It was a time when the path before you was unclear, but you knew in your heart that whatever choice you made would change everything.

Writing about this period brought me back to a time when I was lost, both physically and emotionally. The streets of Yaoundé reflected the uncertainty and fear I carried. I had to learn to trust myself in ways I never imagined. What fears have you had to confront? What hopes have guided you through the darkest times?

Mr. Bernard made me question everything I thought I knew about myself. I encourage you to think about the encounters in your life that have left a lasting impact. Who has changed your story in ways you didn't anticipate?

Consider the decisions that have defined your path. Where are you headed? What choices lie before you?

In sharing my story, I hope you find a connection to your own experiences. What will you uncover about yourself as you continue forward? The answers lie within you.

Chapter 16: The Path Forward

There are times when we look ahead with only hope to guide us. It shows where dreams and reality blend, and the way forward seems fragile. Think about your moments of doubt and determination. Have you ever been unsure if a new direction would lead to success or failure? This story is about fear, courage, and the balance between them. It marks how I see the world and my place in it.

****

The darkness seemed endless, each moment stretching into eternity. I lay awake, my thoughts churning in the stillness. Tomorrow, I will see Mr. Bernard. But even as the thought formed, uncertainty seeped in. Could this be my way out? Or was I chasing a dream that would slip through my fingers just like so many before?

I wanted to believe that tomorrow would bring something better. But I couldn't shake the doubt that clung to me. The streets had been my home for so long; the idea of leaving them behind felt both hopeful and terrifying.

When the first light of dawn began to edge into the sky, I felt a small surge of determination. It wasn't a certainty, but it was enough to push me to my feet. I gathered my few belongings, knowing that while I wasn't sure what the day would bring, I had to see it through. The road ahead was still unknown, but I was ready to face it.

As I approached the Ministry of Finance, every gaze's weight was palpable. I had scrubbed myself clean as best as possible, using the meager water I found, and dressed in the least tattered clothes I had. Yet, I still looked out of place—the pants were old, the shirt was too big, and my shoes had seen better days.

When I finally reached the ministry's entrance, my heart pounded. I approached the reception desk, trying to hold my head high. The woman behind the counter glanced up at me, her eyes narrowing as she took in my appearance.

"What are you doing here?" she asked, her tone laced with suspicion.

For a moment, I hesitated. Then, I pulled out the card Mr. Bernard had given me, holding it out for her to see. "I'm here to see Mr. Bernard," I said, trying to sound confident, even though I could feel the doubt creeping back in.

She scrutinized the card, her eyes narrowing as they flicked back to me. Disbelief clouded her expression as though she suspected this was some cruel joke. Before I could say anything else, a security guard appeared beside me. "You're going to have to leave," he said, his hand on my shoulder, guiding me towards the exit.

My heart sank as we stepped outside. This wasn't how it was supposed to go. I had imagined walking into that building and finding something—hope, a future, maybe even a way out. But instead, here I was, back on the street.

Just as I was about to turn and walk away, I heard a voice call out. "Wait!"

I looked up to see Mr. Bernard, his tall figure striding across the lobby, his expression of recognition. "Let her in," he said to the security guard, who immediately stepped back. "I know who she is."

Mr. Bernard approached, his presence both authoritative and reassuring. "Come with me," he said, and we retraced our steps through the imposing entrance.

The interior of the building was a spectacle of grandeur. Towering glass doors lined the hallways, allowing light streams to dance across the polished marble floors. The ceilings seemed to stretch forever, adding to the grandeur. Everything about the place spoke of power and importance.

As we walked, I couldn't help but be in awe. I had never known this world differed from the streets I had left behind. Mr. Bernard led me through corridors until we reached his office.

His office was vast, dwarfing any room I had ever known. A massive desk dominated one side, impeccably organized with stacks of papers arranged perfectly. Across from the desk, a long table was set up, surrounded by plush chairs. The walls were lined with shelves filled with books—thick volumes that looked like they hadn't been touched in years. There were also games, wooden chess sets, and boxes with intricate designs. The shelves held an entire set of encyclopedias, their spines worn from use, giving the room an air of knowledge and wisdom.

Mr. Bernard gestured for me to sit at the table. "Make yourself comfortable," he said with a smile. "We have much to discuss."

He then called his secretary and asked her to bring food and beverages. Within minutes, a tray of food was delivered to the office. Mr. Bernard invited me to eat, reassuring me that I should take my time while he continued working. He busied himself with papers and documents, but his demeanor was warm.

When he finished, he set his pen down and looked at me. "How are you doing?" he asked.

"I'm doing well," I replied, though my voice was hesitant.

"Did you talk to your grandmother?" he continued, his tone gentle.

This time, I told him everything. I explained how my grandmother lived with my aunt, and told me not to contact him when I went back to see her. But I did it anyway. As I spoke, Mr. Bernard listened intently, his expression thoughtful.

After I finished, he said, "Thank you for telling me the truth. I understand why you did what you did."

He then offered a solution I hadn't expected. "I've arranged for you to stay in a hotel for a week," he said. "During that time, you can find a home—somewhere safe and stable. And once you do, we can bring your grandmother to live with you. Would that be something you'd like?"

I looked at him, almost unable to believe what I was hearing. It was too good to be true. This had to be a dream, a fairytale. Why was he doing this? What was happening? I thought about running momentarily—this was all too strange, too perfect.

But then, I decided to trust the process, to go with the flow, even though it felt surreal.

"Yes," I finally said. "That would be a dream come true."

He smiled warmly. "Then it's settled. We'll make it happen."

As he returned to his desk, I caught a fleeting glimpse of something—an undercurrent of sorrow that briefly clouded his features before vanishing as swiftly as it had appeared. I wondered if something weighed on his mind, but I didn't dare ask.

After I left Mr. Bernard's office, I went to the hotel where he had arranged for me to stay. It was a week of luxury, but I didn't let myself get too comfortable. I knew this was temporary—I needed to find a home.

Each day, I woke up in the softest bed I had ever known, surrounded by silence. I found a real estate agent who knew the city well, and we started looking at properties together. I knew what I wanted—a medium-sized home with three bedrooms and two bathrooms inside. The bathrooms were outside in some homes, a relic of older, traditional designs. But I didn't want that. I wanted everything inside, safe and secure.

We visited several neighborhoods. Bessengue didn't appeal to me. It was too busy, too loud. Bonapriso, with its well-kept streets and manicured lawns, felt almost too perfect, too detached from the life I knew. But when I arrived in Ékounou, I felt something different. The house was beautiful, just what I had been looking for. The neighborhood was quiet, with friendly neighbors. What made Ékounou stand out was that it was close to my grandmother. Living near her was important to me, and that's what made this place feel appealing.

As I walked through the house, I imagined what it would be like to live there with my grandmother. The thought of having a home filled me with joy, fear, and hope.

Once I secured the house, Mr. Bernard helped me enroll at College La Madelena. I received my uniforms, school supplies, and everything else I needed to start this new chapter of my life. Standing in front of the school gates, I felt both excitement and anxiety. This was it—the start of something new.

Yet, as I looked ahead, I wondered if this new beginning would last. And what battles was Mr. Bernard fighting, even as he helped me with mine?

Little did I know, the day was fast approaching when I would return to Ékounou, not alone, but with my grandmother by my side. We would walk out of that house, leaving behind the past. The image of my aunt and her family watching us go, powerless to stop us, brought me anticipation.

For now, I allowed myself to breathe and believe. I will return to Ékounou tomorrow to share the news with my grandmother. Tomorrow, we will begin the next chapter of our lives together. As I drifted to sleep in that soft bed, I held onto the promise of what would come.

Reflection

When faced with uncertainty, did you step forward or retreat into the comfort of the familiar? What would you do if given a chance to rewrite your story, leave behind the shadows of your past, and step into the light of a new beginning? As you ponder these questions, consider Born of Angels and Demons and belief. Even in the darkest times, these forces propel us forward and help us find our way when the path is unclear. Ask yourself: what dreams have you left behind, and what would it take for you to chase them once again?

Reader's Challenge

Now that you've walked with me through this chapter, I challenge you to reflect on a pivotal moment in your life. What choices did you make, and what were the outcomes? Write it down and share your story with others if you feel inspired. Let's create a community of shared experiences and mutual encouragement.

Chapter 17: The Return

Sometimes, the journey forward begins with a step back, a return to places that hold both pain and promise. These moments offer us the chance to revisit our past with new strength, reclaim what was lost, and shape a new future from the remnants of what it once was.

This chapter is not just about a return to a physical place but a return to oneself, to the resilience and strength forged in the fires of adversity. It is a moment of reckoning, where the echoes of the past meet the possibilities of the future. As you read, consider the moments in your own life where you've had to return to the source of your pain, not to dwell on it but to transform it into a steppingstone for something greater.

Let this chapter be a reminder that every return carries the seeds of renewal within it and that within the heart of every struggle lies the potential for growth, healing, and, ultimately, freedom.

****

The morning sun barely managed to break through the thick clouds as I left the hotel where Mr. Bernard had arranged for me to stay. Each step toward Ékounou felt closer to a new life I had only dared to imagine. This day wasn't like the others—it was the day I would return to Aunt Régine's house, where my grandmother had been living, a place that had symbolized fear and hardship. But this time, I wasn't returning empty-handed. I carried with me the promise of a better life, not just for myself but for my grandmother—the woman who had been my refuge during the most challenging times.

As I approached the house, memories resurfaced—nights on the streets, the hunger, the loneliness. But today was different. Today, I had something to offer—a way out.

The door creaked as I knocked, a sound so familiar yet now filled with finality. When it opened, there she was—my grandmother. Her face, lined with years of struggle, softened as our eyes met. Despite everything, her gaze still held that warmth that had always been my haven.

For a moment, we just stood there, silent. She pulled me into her arms with a smile that reached her eyes. As she embraced me, the weight of the past months lifted, replaced by the comfort of being home.

"I have something to tell you," I whispered, my voice trembling under the weight of the news I was about to share. "We're free, Grandmother. We have a home. I'm back in school. We don't have to live like this anymore."

Her grip tightened as if she needed to hold on to something real. She pulled back slightly, searching my eyes to understand what I was saying. Her voice was thick with disbelief, relief, and hope when she finally spoke.

"Tell me everything," she said, guiding me inside.

We sat in the small living room, and I told her everything. Despite her warnings, I confessed that I had seen Mr. Bernard. I explained how he had seen something in me, something worth nurturing, and he had enrolled me in school, found us a home, and even arranged for a monthly allowance so we could live comfortably.

As I spoke, I watched her closely. Relief washed over her, but there was still concern in her eyes. Yet, as the reality of our new life began to sink in, her expression softened. Her eyes filled with tears, and without a word, she fell to her knees, clasping her hands together.

"Oh, Lord," she whispered, her voice trembling. "I thank you. You've heard my prayers. You've answered them. Thank you."

Her words were more than just a prayer—they were a hymn of gratitude that filled the room. She stayed there on her knees, tears streaming down her face, giving thanks to God for the miracle that had finally arrived.

I stood there, watching her, my heart swelling. This was more than just relief—it resulted from years of faith, of holding on when everything seemed lost. Her prayers, whispered in the darkest nights, had been answered.

When she finally rose to her feet, she looked at me with pride and love. "You've done something incredible, my child," she said softly. "You've stepped toward a future that once seemed impossible."

Her words wrapped around me like a blanket, comforting and reassuring. This was no longer about surviving but building a life where we could finally be free from fear and uncertainty.

"Come, let's get your things," I said, standing up and offering her my hand. "It's time to leave this place behind."

As we gathered her few belongings, I felt finality, a liberation beyond just packing a bag. The small bundle she packed held little more than the essentials, but it symbolized so much more—it was the last tie to a life of struggle, the last step before we fully embraced our new future.

As we left Aunt Régine's house, I glanced back again. A mix of emotions welled within me—relief, joy, and a quiet sadness for the life we were leaving behind. But I knew what lay ahead was far more significant—a new chapter where we could finally be free.

Hand in hand, we walked away from the past toward a future that was ours to create. The path ahead was still uncertain, but it was filled with possibilities for the first time in a long while.

Our days soon settled into a rhythm that brought the stability we longed for. Every morning, just as the first light of dawn appeared, my grandmother would prepare to leave for her farm. The farm wasn't thriving as it once had, but it remained where she found purpose. She would leave early, her movements deliberate, as if tending to the earth was her way of staying grounded.

I would watch her go, feeling deeply grateful that we had come this far. I would prepare for school, slipping into the routine Mr. Bernard had made possible. School was a new world for me—a place where I could focus on my studies, where the future seemed like something within reach.

When I returned home in the afternoons, the smell of dinner would greet me at the door. Despite the weariness of her day, my grandmother always had a meal prepared—a simple meal that filled our small home with warmth. We would sit together at the table, and in these quiet moments, she would share her wisdom with me.

One evening, as we finished our meal, she looked at me with wise eyes and began speaking. "Cara," she said, "I want to tell you a story about persistence."

I leaned in, eager to hear her next lesson.

"There was once a king," she began, "who found himself on the run after being defeated in battle. Disheartened, he took refuge in a cave, where he sat, pondering whether to give up his throne. Sitting there, he noticed a tiny spider trying to spin a web across the cave entrance. The spider kept trying to attach its web to the rock, but it fell apart each time.

The king watched as the spider tried repeatedly, never giving up. Finally, on its seventh attempt, the spider anchored the web. Inspired by the spider's persistence, the king realized that he, too, must not give up after a few failures. Renewed in spirit, he left the cave, rallied his troops, and eventually reclaimed his throne.

Cara, this story teaches us the value of persistence. No matter how often we fail, it's important to keep trying because success usually comes to those who refuse to give up."

I absorbed her words, understanding that they were as much about our journey as they were about the king's.

Another night, after a long day at school, my grandmother shared another story with me. We sat by the small fire she had built to warm our home, the light flickering on the walls.

"Cara," she began, "I want to tell you a story about unity and strength."

I leaned in closer, feeling the warmth of the fire and her presence.

"There was once an old man," she said, "with three sons who were always quarreling. On his deathbed, he called them together and handed each other a stick, asking them to break it. Each son quickly broke their stick. The older man tied three sticks together and gave them to his sons, asking them to break the bundle. None of the sons could break the bundled sticks despite their best efforts.

The old man said, 'My sons if you remain united like this bundle of sticks, no one will be able to break you. But if you are divided, you will be as easily broken as those single sticks.'

This fable is about the strength that comes from unity and working together. It is a lesson about the power of family and community, reminding us that together we are stronger than we are alone."

Her words resonated deeply, especially after all the challenges we had faced. They reminded us that, despite everything, we were stronger together.

On one quiet evening, as we cleared the dishes from the table, my grandmother looked thoughtful, as if something was weighing on her mind.

"There are times," she began softly, "when even the strongest bonds can be tested, and sometimes, those tests come from within the very heart of our families."

I paused, sensing a deeper meaning in her words. She rarely spoke in such a cryptic manner, and it made me feel uneasy.

"Cara," she continued, "there was once a small pebble at the foot of a towering mountain. The mountain was admired by all who passed by. The pebble felt insignificant next to the mountain and lamented, 'I am just a tiny pebble, and no one notices me. The mountain is so grand and important, while I am nothing.'

One day, a storm came, and the mountain was struck by lightning, causing a landslide. The mountain began to crumble, and large rocks tumbled down. But the little pebble remained where it was, untouched by the storm.

After the storm passed, people came to see the damage. They noticed that, despite the mountain's grandeur, it had crumbled in the face of adversity. But the little pebble, though small, had endured.

Cara, this fable teaches us that even the smallest have strength and value. It's a reminder that true resilience isn't always about size or power; sometimes, it's about enduring quietly through life's challenges."

I nodded, but something in her tone made me wonder if she was trying to tell me something more. My grandmother had a way of weaving deeper meanings into her stories, often hinting at things yet to come. I sensed an unease, a quiet foreboding that settled in the back of my mind.

As we continued our routine in the following days, I noticed small things that didn't quite add up, like how my grandmother would glance towards Aunt Régine's house with a furrowed brow or the hushed conversations she had with other women in the market. There was tension in the air, something unsaid but felt like the pressure building before a storm.

But life went on, as it always did. We continued to find peace in our simple days, even as I couldn't shake the feeling that something was coming that would test the strength of our newly built life.

One night, that feeling came to a head as the wind picked up, howling through the trees outside our tiny home. I lay in bed, staring at the ceiling, unable to shake the impending change. My grandmother's earlier words echoed in my mind, a quiet warning I couldn't ignore.

Just as I drifted off to sleep, there was a knock at the door. It was hesitant, almost fearful. My heart jumped as I slipped out of bed and crept to the door. When I opened it, I saw my cousin Syntiche standing there, drenched from the rain, her small frame shivering from the cold. For a moment, I just stared at her, my mind racing. What is she doing here? Why is she alone on my doorstep in the middle of a storm?

Without thinking, I shut the door, my heart pounding. I leaned against it, trying to calm the whirlwind of thoughts suddenly taking over. Why was she here? Should I let her in? The storm outside raged on, the wind howling as the rain beat against the windows. I could feel the weight of the decision pressing down on me, my mind a chaotic mix of fear, anger, and confusion.

I thought about everything Aunt Régine had ever said to me—how she had told me I would never amount to anything, that I was nothing. I remember her saying, "School isn't for you.

Why should I waste time or money on you going to school? A thing like you will never amount to anything." Her words cut deep, significantly, when she added, "If you ever see me coming to ask for help, don't help me. But I don't see that scenario ever happening because you're nothing. You will never do anything, never be anything."

And now, her daughter was standing on my doorstep, seeking refuge. The irony wasn't lost on me. Part of me wanted to leave her out there, to let her feel just a fraction of the pain I had endured. But another part of me hesitated, shaped by my grandmother's unwavering kindness. What would she do in this situation?

Taking a deep breath, I opened the door again, this time more slowly. When I did, I saw Syntiche and the rest of them—my Aunt Régine, her face pale and streaked with tears, and her other children huddled together in the rain. They were soaked, their clothes clinging to them as they stood there, looking as lost and desperate as I had felt many times before.

"Cara," Aunt Régine whispered, her voice barely audible over the storm, "I—I didn't know where else to go."

I stood there, frozen in the doorway, the storm raging around us. Seeing them—so vulnerable, so desperate—brought a flood of emotions. But one thought, clear as day, echoed in my mind: this woman had once told me I would never amount to anything, that I was nothing. And now, she was standing at my door, seeking refuge.

The tension hung as I grappled with what to do next.

Reflection

1. **Confronting the Past:** This chapter delves into the decisive act of returning to a place of past pain, not to relieve the hurt but to reclaim your power. Think about a time when you had to revisit a painful memory or place. How did that experience shape you? Did it offer you a chance to heal, or did it open new wounds? How did you navigate those emotions?

2. **The Power of Resilience:** Resilience isn't about enduring hardship—it's about transforming that hardship into strength. As you reflect on the challenges this chapter faces, consider your journey. Where have you shown resilience in your life? How has your past adversity fueled your growth?

3. **The Role of Gratitude:** Gratitude plays a significant role in this chapter, with the character's grandmother expressing deep thankfulness for the blessings that have come after an extended period of suffering. How has gratitude played a role in your life during challenging times? How can you cultivate a more grateful perspective, even amid challenges?

4. **Forgiveness and Moving Forward:** The chapter touches on the tension between past hurt and the need to move forward, particularly in the relationship with Aunt Régine. Have you ever struggled to forgive someone who caused you pain? How did that struggle affect your ability

to move forward? What does forgiveness look like, and how can it free you from the past?

5. **The Promise of Renewal:** Returning to a place of pain with newfound hope can be a transformative experience. Reflect on moments in your life where you've seen potential in situations that once seemed hopeless. How did that shift in perspective change your path? How can you apply that mindset to the current challenges you face?

Reflection

Reflecting on this chapter of my life, I am reminded of the incredible power of facing the past head-on. Returning to Ékounou, to the very place that held so much pain for me, was not easy. But it was necessary. It was a journey to reclaim my physical place, sense of self, dignity, and future. In those moments, I realized that true strength isn't just about moving forward; it's about being willing to go back, confront what haunts you, and transform it into something that empowers you.

The resilience I found within myself during this time is something I carry to this day. It's a reminder that no matter how many times life knocks you down, there's always the possibility of standing back up, stronger and more determined than before. This chapter of my life taught me that resilience is about survival and thriving in the face of adversity.

Gratitude played a massive role in my journey. Seeing my grandmother's reaction, her tears of joy, and hearing her prayers of thanks were moments that anchored me. They reminded me that even in the darkest times, there is always something to be thankful for and that gratitude can be a source of strength that carries you through the most challenging days.

Forgiveness, however, was a more complicated matter. Standing at that door, faced with the very people who had caused me so much pain, I struggled with the decision of whether to help or to turn away. But in the end, I chose to let go of the past, not for them, but for myself. Forgiveness, I have learned, is not about excusing the behavior of others but about freeing yourself from the burden of anger and bitterness.

Finally, this chapter represents a renewal for both my grandmother and me. It was a time when we took the broken pieces of our past and began to build something new, something better. This experience taught me that within every struggle lies the seed of renewal and that it's up to us to nurture and allow it to grow.

Chapter 18: The Storm's Arrival and Aftermath

The arrival of my siblings brought new challenges to our already crowded home, pushing us to our limits. With more people under one roof, we faced problematic decisions and needed solutions that could help us all move forward. During this time, I encountered figures from my past, reminding me of the connections and responsibilities that have shaped my life. Throughout these changes, I sought guidance and understanding, knowing that the road ahead would require strength and clear thinking.

****

The maelstrom that night was unlike anything I had ever experienced. Thunder roared through the air like a ferocious beast while lightning slashed across the sky, exposing the surroundings in fleeting bursts. The wind howled, rattling the windows and causing the entire house to tremble. Rain hammered relentlessly as if the heavens were intent on obliterating everything in its path.

I sat by the window, gazing out at the raging elements. Each crash of thunder sent a jolt through me, but it wasn't just the chaos outside that disturbed me. The unrest within my mind, swirling memories and fears, created a vortex that reflected the one beyond the glass.

A sudden knock on the door broke the fragile calm. My heart skipped a beat, and for a moment, I hesitated, torn between apprehension and curiosity. Who could be out in such weather? Dear me, it seemed impossible, yet the knocking persisted, becoming increasingly urgent with every moment.

When I finally opened the door, the sight before me was startling. There, drenched and trembling, stood Syntiche—my young cousin. Her wide eyes reflected a dread that swirled like a hurricane. Her clothes clung to her petite frame, soaked by the ceaseless rain, and she looked up at me as if I were her only hope.

For a moment, I was frozen, the reality of the situation crashing over me like a wave. The thunder outside gradually faded as a whirlwind of feelings stirred within me. Memories of Aunt Régine's harsh words came flooding back—how she had told me I was nothing, how she had declared I would never amount to anything, and how she had vowed that if she ever came to me for help, I should turn her away. And yet, here she was, standing at my doorstep, seeking the very refuge she had once denied me.

Without thinking, I shut the door and leaned against it, trying to conceal the jarring truth that had just struck me. My mind spiraled, thoughts clashing in a tumultuous whirl. What was I meant to do? How was I supposed to react? The turbulence outside persisted, mirroring the confusion and conflict within my soul.

I opened the door again. I saw them all—my aunt Régine, drenched from the rain, her once proud demeanor now worn and diminished. Behind her stood her children—Patou, Mame, Papi, Mami, Syntiche, and my cousin Alain, Uncle Baboulek's son. They all huddled together, their faces etched with sorrow and resignation, looking like a family broken by more than just hardship.

I waged a battle within myself; the urge to surrender to bitterness and resentment was strong. But then my grandmother's words came to me: "Always choose kindness, Cara. Please allow them to enter."

"Come in," I said quietly, stepping aside to let them pass. They moved past me, leaving a trail of water on the floor. The room felt heavy with the weight of everything that had happened between us. I could sense their fear and need for shelter beneath it all.

When they arrived, my grandmother left her room and saw the scene before her. She approached me, placing a hand on my shoulder.

"You did the right thing," she whispered. "You have a good heart. I'm proud of you."

My aunt then confided in her, sharing how her husband had left her for another woman, leaving her with no money, no resources, and nowhere to go. Despite the strained relationship, my grandmother couldn't turn her away. Knowing it wasn't just for one night, we prepared a spare room for my aunt, her children, and my cousin Alain, ready for them to stay until a permanent solution could be found.

Days turned weeks and weeks into months as they adjusted to our already crowded home. The house now felt chaotic. Mornings were incredibly hectic—everyone bumping into each other in the narrow hallway, waiting for their turn to use the bathroom. The scramble for water rushed bathing, filling buckets, and emptying quickly. Breakfast was no different; with too many hands reaching for too little food, the kitchen crowded as everyone tried to prepare a meal. The strain on our resources was evident: water ran low, food had to be stretched, and every task became hard. The home, which used to be calm, is now busy with ongoing activities, leaving little space for rest or quiet.

I often received invitations from friends at school or neighbors, which I usually declined. But eventually, I started accepting them, using these outings to escape the noise at home and find some peace elsewhere. One day, I went shopping with my friends, and as we browsed the shops, we came across a vendor's stand filled with posters, T-shirts, and CDs. The man behind the stand caught my eye—tall, skinny, dark-skinned, youthful energy. He looked about 18 or 19 years old. As I picked up a CD, he looked at me and asked, "Aren't you Cara, the girl from Ngaoundéré? Your father was the treasurer of finance, wasn't he? And you had a big house with a giant gate."

I quickly denied it, shaking my head. "You must be mistaken," I replied.

But the man didn't seem convinced. "All right, if you say so," he said, though his eyes suggested otherwise. Curious, I asked his name. He hesitated before answering, "Elso." The name was instantly familiar. We attended kindergarten through fifth grade together. Elso was always at the top of the class, consistently placing first, while I usually ranked within the top five. I remember our academic rivalry well.

Elso was three or four years older than me. Still, in Cameroon, particularly in villages where education is limited, it's common for students of different ages to be in the same grade. Children often start school at various stages due to family responsibilities or lack of access, so older students like Elso could be in the same class as younger ones. Not wanting him to sense my thoughts, I quickly signaled to my friends, and we walked away. His familiarity with my past in Ngaoundéré stirred up memories I had tried to bury. In the following weeks, I found myself drawn back to his stand—not just out of wonder but because he represented a link to a part of my life that felt distant. My friends and I became regular visitors, and though I continued to deny my identity, my interactions with him made me wonder if I could truly escape the past that had shaped me. Little did I know this connection would grow into something more significant, eventually playing a more prominent role in my life.

At home, another disruption loomed as we adjusted to a new rhythm. My biological mother, who had moved to Yokadouma with her new husband, Henry, was facing troubles of her own. Henry, who had two children with my mother, Noël and Christelle, became increasingly hostile toward my siblings, Babou and Rose, believing their father, Daniel, should take responsibility for them. Henry demanded that they be sent away. My mother sent them back to live with us.

The arrival of my siblings was bittersweet. They looked malnourished and worried, their eyes hollow from their ordeals. Babou, tall and skinny, had a quiet demeanor that spoke of burdens carried at an early age. Rose had a similar look, appearing fragile as she clung to my grandmother. The first thing they did when they arrived was eat. My grandmother fed them Ndolé, Bongo Tchobi, and Miondo—traditional Cameroonian meals. Ndolé is a dish with bitter leaves, nuts, and meat or fish, frequently served with plantains or cassava. Bongo Tchobi is a steamed plantain pudding, and Miondo is made from fermented cassava, typically served as a side dish.

In the morning, my grandmother and Aunt Régine would cook breakfast for everyone. After we had eaten, we would go our separate ways—my grandmother went to her farm, my aunt's children and I went to school, leaving Babou and Rose at home. I started wondering about the future and how I could help them get to school. At that time in Cameroon, schooling was not accessible. Families had to pay for tuition, uniforms, and supplies. Some students would even sit on the floor without a proper chair. Education was a significant financial burden, especially for low-income families like ours, and it made me worry about how we could afford to send Babou and Rose to school.

That afternoon, after I got home from school and finished my homework, I talked to my grandmother about my concerns for Babou and Rose's future and education. We discussed our financial situation and how we could manage it. I told her I planned to speak with Mr. Bernard, and she agreed it was a good idea.

Later that day, I went to the Ministry of Finance. When I entered Mr. Bernard's office, he greeted me warmly, but his expression changed when he saw the worry on my face. "What brings you here today, Cara?" he asked. I explained everything—the arrival of my siblings, the presence of my aunt and her children, and how it was all becoming too much. I told him I wanted to enroll Babou and Rose in school and needed more support.

After a moment, Mr. Bernard leaned back in his chair and said, "I admire your commitment to helping your siblings. I'll increase your allowance to ensure you can provide for them, but I also think it's time your aunt found a more permanent solution. Your home is overcrowded, and it's unfair to you or your grandmother to continue like this."

The idea of asking my aunt to leave was difficult, but deep down, I knew it was necessary. The situation was unsustainable, and something would have to change sooner.

I sat with my grandmother in the quiet kitchen. I told her about my conversation with Mr. Bernard and concerns about the packed house. We agreed that my aunt needed to find an approach, as we couldn't continue like this. My grandmother said she understood and would talk to her daughter to see what could be done.

Several days had passed since that conversation, and I wondered if my grandmother had spoken to my aunt. That morning, before school, I asked if she had discussed things with her. My grandmother confirmed she had and said we would wait to see what would happen next. It didn't take long for things to change. My aunt met a man named Edward and soon informed my grandmother that their relationship had become severe. They planned to move in together within weeks, and the tension in the household started to ease. Excited about the fresh start, she quickly packed her belongings, and the atmosphere improved.

Each evening, after dinner, my grandmother would tell us stories, and those were some of the best moments we shared. We would gather around, listening closely as she spoke.

She told one story about a young woman who had to fetch water daily from a river far from her village. She carried a large pot on her head, careful not to spill any water on the way back. One day, she tripped, and the pot fell, shattering and spilling the water. The young woman felt devastated, but an elder in the village told her, "Do not cry over what is lost. Sometimes, things break so that something new can be made from the pieces." The young woman gathered the broken parts and used them to create a mosaic that became the village's pride, a reminder that something valuable can be made even when things fall apart.

Another story was about two birds. One bird could fly high, soaring through the sky, while the other could only hop from branch to branch. The flying bird saw the grounded bird as useless because it couldn't soar. But as the grounded bird moved among the branches, it discovered nests hidden deep within the trees, treasures that the flying bird had overlooked. They both realized that while the sky offers one view, the ground provides another. They learned to appreciate each other's unique perspective, understanding that everyone has a role to play.

These fables taught me about finding value in grim times, embracing what makes us different, and the importance of strength, character, and kindness.

Reflection

In this part of my journey, I face the realities of responsibility and family dynamics. The arrival of my siblings and the extended stay of my aunt and her children put a strain on our crowded home, making me realize the limits of what we could manage. My conversation with Mr. Bernard pushed me to see the need for change, even when it was hard.

My unexpected encounter with Elso, a figure from my past, made me question whether I could genuinely leave behind where I came from. His presence reminded me of the past I had tried to move on from, but it also suggested that some connections might still need to be resolved.

The tales my grandmother shared each evening offered guidance, showing me that there is always room for growth, even in challenging times. These tales reflected the struggles I was dealing with—learning to manage the tensions at home and the uncertainty of what lay ahead.

This period marks a time of change and learning. It's about understanding the need for difficult decisions and the lessons we carry with us from the chronicles and experiences that shape us.

Chapter 19: Navigating Change

This section explores a crucial time in my life with significant changes and tough decisions. It was a period when I dealt with personal and external difficulties, trying to stay true to myself through choices and the support I sought. I discovered the importance of remaining committed to what I believe was right.

Life often requires us to balance choices with the secrets we keep at a crossroads. I felt what had been done. There was hope and a chance to carve out a new direction, even with obstacles.

****

The day my aunt Régine and her children left, I stood at the door with my grandmother, watching them part their belongings into Edouard's trunk. When the vehicle was packed, I heard the final lock close on everything related to them. They waved goodbye and drove away, vanishing down the road. I said out loud, "Thank God they're gone."

For a moment, I wondered if I would see her again and hoped she would find the happiness she was seeking.

It was just my grandmother, Rose, Babou, and me now. Our routine became stable, and responsibilities settled into place. I prepared each morning for the day, preparing Rose and Babou for school. I ensured they showered, had breakfast, dressed, and had their backpacks prepared before leaving. I cared for them at home and did my best to keep up appearances. I became more protective, pouring all my energy into being the best sister and second mother.

Caring for Rose and Babou was rewarding and overwhelming during this period. While I was determined to give them the care they needed, I couldn't ignore the responsibility on me. I was still a kid, yet I was a protector and caregiver. With my aging grandmother unable to look after me the way I needed, the only person left to help my siblings was me. I often felt exhausted and alone. I wanted to be strong for them, but sometimes, I wished someone could care for me. It was tough.

I continued spending my days with my friends Yolande and Armandine. School became my focus as I realized how much I wanted to change my life. I spent more energy studying, working hard on my homework, and practicing math, science, and chemistry with them.

One afternoon, we decided to meet for a study session, and as I was on my way to their homes, I came across a narrow spot where only one person could pass at a time. As I approached, I noticed someone coming from the other side. It was Elso. We reached the exact moment, and one of us had to move. He looked at me and asked, "You're the girl from Ngaoundéré, Cara, right? You're Cara."

I quickly replied, "It's not me. You're mistaken. You're probably thinking of someone else. I'm sorry; I have to go."

He stepped aside, letting me pass. I hurried along to Yolande and Armandine's place, ready to focus on our homework.

After finishing my homework, I returned and saw Elso again, waiting on the other side. As I approached, he smiled and said, "We meet again. Why don't you admit it? I know you're the girl from Ngaoundéré. What are you hiding?"

I looked down, unable to meet his eyes. He continued, "It's okay, you can talk to me. I remember you. You lived in a villa, had a chauffeur, and your father was respected. What happened?"

I finally said, "I am Cara from Ngaoundéré."

He nodded, "I knew it. Why didn't you tell me?"

"It's a long story, and it's hard to talk about everything now," I replied.

Elso didn't push any further. "I understand," he said. "I live nearby with my family in a compound. I have a private room, and you can visit anytime. No one will know."

We kept talking, and I shared what had happened to my father—how he was arrested and is now in prison in Yaoundé, Kondengui. I told him how I had been homeless for a while, but Bernard found me, adopted me, and took care of me, my siblings, and my grandmother. We lived in Ékounou, and I was going to Colège de la Madeleine.

Elso smiled. "That's the first time I noticed you—you passed by my stand, but you were always with your friends, so I never had a chance to approach you. I'm thrilled we met here."

He expressed his desire to stay in touch, and I agreed. From that day on, I spent it with him whenever I had free time after school. Sometimes, I'd visit his stand in Yaoundé Central and help him before heading home.

After that, Elso brought much joy into my life. As I cared for my siblings and aging grandmother and worked hard to stay in the top three in my class, being with Elso became a bright spot. We talked about everything, and he would send me gifts—clothes and other things. He was very generous, and we often took long walks together.

During those walks, he opened up about his religion. He was Muslim and very strict in his practice, praying five times a day and following the restrictions of his faith. We were careful about my visits because we didn't want his family to know. As Christians, our relationship could have caused problems. At that time in Cameroon, relationships between Muslims and Christians were complicated due to profound cultural and religious differences.

Islam and Christianity were the two dominant religions, and while people from both communities coexisted, interfaith relationships were often frowned upon, especially in traditional families. In Muslim families, marrying outside of the faith was considered not only rare but also forbidden. For Christians, especially devout ones, marrying a Muslim could lead to ostracism, as there were fears about conversion and the influence of Islamic traditions, which could conflict with Christian values.

In Cameroon, these religious divides went beyond personal beliefs. There were societal expectations and strong family pressures. Marriages were often arranged within the same religion to ensure the continuity of beliefs and traditions. A relationship like ours, between a Muslim and a Christian, wasn't just viewed as an individual choice—it was seen as something that could disrupt the social fabric of the community. Families feared such unions would lead to religious conflict or force one partner to abandon their faith.

For Elso and me, this meant that even though we cared for each other, we had to keep our relationship hidden. His family, being strict Muslims, would not have accepted our friendship, much less anything more. If they had known, there would have been serious consequences, perhaps even forcing him to end our connection. On my side, as a Christian, I knew my family wouldn't understand either. The cultural gap between our religions made everything we shared beautiful and fragile.

The idea of marriage between us, even in the future, was almost unthinkable. At the time, interfaith marriages were rare in Cameroon, and both religious communities often faced opposition. Such relationships were seen as a threat to religious purity, and both families would likely intervene to stop them before they could grow into something serious. This pressure added another layer of difficulty to our bond, making us careful about every interaction, knowing we had to navigate the expectations of two very different worlds.

Elso and I started talking more about our dreams as our relationship grew. I was determined to become a doctor and worked hard for that goal. Elso had a different vision—he dreamed of going to the United States. He believed that if we went there, we could escape the pressure from our families and the weight of our religious differences. He thought we could live freely and make our dreams come true in a new place.

The idea of leaving everything behind and starting fresh in the U.S. felt exciting and almost magical at the time. We would talk about it often, imagining what life would be like abroad, free from the expectations that held us back. It was a dream that brought hope and excitement to our conversations.

We continued dating, but after a while, I started feeling sick. Getting to school became difficult, and I couldn't keep my meals down. It felt off, and I was worried about telling my grandmother. Even though we had a close relationship, I hadn't shared anything about Elso with her, so I kept this to myself.

Instead, I talked to Yolande and Armandine, the only ones I could trust. They asked me how I felt, trying to figure out what was happening. They asked if I had pain in my breasts, if I'd missed my period, and if I had headaches or heartburn. I answered their questions, and I knew what it all meant deep down.

A few days later, I confirmed what we had suspected. I was pregnant.

I spent my days and evenings thinking about what to do next. My mind raced with thoughts of the future, my dreams, and the life I had envisioned. With this living creature growing inside me, everything felt uncertain. The idea of escaping to a place free from all the pressures had once seemed like the perfect solution, but I had to face the reality of making decisions that would shape my life.

I couldn't help but think about my mother. My grandmother had shared stories of when she was in a similar situation, pregnant with me. I wondered how she had felt back then. Did she feel the same way I do now? And why was I walking down the same road? She had been in junior high, just like me. The thought that this was repeating itself terrified me.

This wasn't what I wanted for my life. I had bigger dreams of becoming a doctor and having a hopeful future. I didn't want to end up like my mother, trapped in a cycle I was so determined to break.

I met Yolande and Armandine again, and they could tell something was happening. They asked how I felt and whether I had decided what to do next. That's when they suggested I could have an abortion. They said they knew someone who could help, and it would be quick and simple—done and over with.

As I listened, my mind went back to my mom. I remembered how she left me when I was just two years old, maybe because she felt the same pressure I was feeling now. Maybe she was just like I was; scared of being a mom so young.

But I also thought about how hard my life had been. I didn't want my baby—whether it was a boy or girl—to face the same pain. To me, having an abortion felt like killing someone. It wasn't something I could bring myself to do.

So, I told them no. That day, I made up my mind: I would have this baby, even if it meant pushing my dreams aside for now.

After deciding to have my child, I couldn't stop thinking about why I was following the same path as my mother. History was repeating itself, and I needed to understand why. Was this my fate? Or had I been conditioned to walk the same road without realizing it? What was leading me to go through the same struggles?

I knew I needed to dig deeper. I needed to understand my mother—what really happened from her perspective. I had only heard pieces of her story through my grandmother, but now I needed to hear it from her. I needed to know who she was and why she made her choices. And not just her—I also needed to learn about my biological father. I needed to find out more about where I came from.

And then there was Elso. He wasn't my husband, and with the tension between being a Christian and him being a Muslim, I knew we faced our challenges. Understanding where I came from felt like the key to breaking the cycle; I seemed to be trapped in it.

As these thoughts circled in my mind, I knew my next step had to be reaching out to my parents. There were too many unanswered questions; understanding them could help me move forward. My decision to become a mother was already made, but now it was time to face my past, uncover the truths that had shaped my life, and figure out how to break the cycle.

<u>Reflection</u>

In this chapter, I navigate the pressure from those around me while focusing on what matters most. I found holding on to my values was key, even when the road was difficult. The journey wasn't easy, but staying true to what I believed was essential.

Looking back, I see that life has many twists and turns. It reminds me that our choices shape who we are, even when the way forward isn't what we expected. We must stay aligned with what we value most. The experience showed how societal expectations can strain relationships and how hard it is to balance personal desires with outside pressures. I learned that understanding the consequences of my actions was key to moving forward.

Chapter 20: The Weight of Inheritance

The road to Yokadouma wasn't just about covering miles. It was a journey into my past, a chance to face the questions that had stayed with me for years. I was about to meet the woman who gave me life but had always been distant. Something inside me was changing. What would I find behind the doors that kept us apart? Would this meeting answer me or make things even more confusing? No matter what, I knew it was a step I had to take to understand where I came from and figure out where I was going.

****

My grandmother's silence felt different now. Though she hadn't asked me anything, she was piecing things together. I couldn't hide the truth much longer.

One evening, as we sat together, I spoke. "Grandmother, I have something to tell you."

She turned to me. "What is it, child?"

"I'm pregnant."

She was surprised but stayed quiet for a moment.

"I had a feeling," she finally said. "It's good that you are following your path. It won't be easy, but you are strong. And I'll be here."

Later, I met with Elso. He had been asking questions for a while, and it was time to tell him everything.

"I need to talk to you."

"What's going on?"

"I'm pregnant."

He looked at me for a moment. "It's going to be okay. We'll figure this out."

"There's something else. I need to see my mother. I need to understand where I come from, and she's the only one who can give me those answers."

"If that's what you need, then go. I'll be here when you get back. Everything will be fine."

This journey wasn't just about my pregnancy but about discovering who I was. The road to Yokadouma was calling me, and I knew I had to take it.

It wasn't just about walking away from my grandmother when I left. Rose, Babou, and Bernard stayed behind as I took my first step toward Yokadouma.

The town of Yokadouma appeared slowly on the horizon, with small houses and narrow streets. The scene felt familiar, but only from the stories I had heard, not from experience. As I got closer, everything around me seemed still. I walked through the street, each step bringing me nearer to my mother's house. It was smaller than I expected as if it were hidden from the world. My heartbeat was faster, and my mind raced ahead to the door. There were so many things I wanted to say, questions I had practiced over and over, but now, standing at the door, I wasn't sure how to start or what my first word would be.

The long-awaited moment had arrived, and it felt overwhelming. I raised my hand to knock but stopped just before touching the wood. Before I could decide, the door opened slightly, and there she stood. She looked at me, then at my growing belly. Without saying a word, she stepped aside, letting me in. I followed her into the house, where she made space for me. She moved Noël and Christelle, my half-siblings, together to free up a small bed for me. I couldn't speak that night, and the silence lasted until the next day. Even when I met her husband, Henry, at breakfast, the words stayed stuck.

The days passed. Then, days became months. Afternoons outside, evenings at the table, then back to bed. It became routine, and the days blurred together. During that time, I watched my mother closely. She lived as the third wife, something I didn't understand. Polygamy is recognized and accepted in Cameroon, where a man can have multiple wives. My mother shared her husband with two other women. I noticed how she often took a submissive role, always apologizing in arguments and never standing up for herself. It seemed like she had accepted that her needs didn't come first, a reality for many women in marriages like hers.

As I prepared to return to Yaoundé, I kept searching for the right moment to ask her about her life as a child, what happened to her, and why she left me. But I couldn't get those questions out. It was as if I was paralyzed, unable to say the things I had been rehearsing.

As we sat outside one afternoon, I finally asked her about my father. I needed to know who he was. She didn't know where he had gone and suggested I return to Douala to speak to a neighbor named Samuel, who could tell me the truth about him. That was all she offered, and with that, I knew it was time to leave.

That night, as I packed my bag after speaking with my mother, my contractions started. In our culture, it was common to give birth at home, especially with the support of family. Going to the hospital wasn't always the first option, and many women had their babies with the help of relatives. My mother stepped in to help when my contractions lasted through the night.

By the next day, I was exhausted, but when the sun set again, my daughter was born at home, with my mother there to guide me through it.

The moment she arrived, everything changed. The pain from my childhood faded as I held her close, this small presence resting against me. Her eyes, still adjusting to the light, looked around as if searching for something familiar. I wondered if she could answer the questions that still lingered about my place in life. Looking at her, I felt a bond like nothing I had ever known. This fragile being depended entirely on me, and with that came a deep resolve.

My future and hers would not follow the same path as my mother's. I had to create something different, where she would never doubt her worth or experience the abandonment that had shaped my early years.

Afterward, my mother was there, but she kept her distance. She helped when needed, bringing food, cleaning, and watching over my daughter when I needed rest, but we never connected emotionally. There was an unspoken bond between us, a shared experience of motherhood, yet we lived our lives differently. Henry stayed on the sidelines, offering help when it suited him but mostly letting us manage independently. The wives, who had initially shown some interest, soon returned to their usual routines, leaving me to navigate this period alone.

As time passed, I started thinking more about what to do next. The visit to Douala to find Samuel and learn the truth about my father was still in the back of my mind, but now, with my daughter in my life, the choices felt more complicated. I couldn't just leave. I had to think of her well-being, too. When she slept with me, I would reflect on the future. Much was still unclear, but I knew one thing—I had to find a way to provide for her and give her the life I always wanted. This was my chance to break the cycle, to make sure she never felt the loss that had shaped my childhood.

One day, as I prepared to leave, my mother approached me with an unexpected offer. She asked if I needed help. When I asked what she meant, she suggested something that caught me off guard.

"You're still young," she said. "You can leave your daughter with me and go live your life. You can continue to do whatever you want. I'll take care of her."

Considering who my mother had been, the same woman who abandoned me, her offer felt unexpected. How could she now suggest taking care of my daughter after all the years apart? I questioned her motives. Did she genuinely want to help, or was this another way to step back from responsibility? I had fought to create a different life for my daughter, one where she would never experience the abandonment I had known.

The more I thought about it, the more confident I became that I was about to relive my mother's life, the one I'd known as a child. This clarity led me to decline her offer and begin my return to Yaoundé, focused on creating a path for myself and my daughter.

Reflection

"There's a strange tension in trying to reconcile the stories I've told myself with the reality I now face. Growing up, I constructed my perception of who my mother was and the reasons behind the choices she made. Filling in the blanks with my ideas was more accessible than facing what I didn't understand. But now, being here in her world, I'm struck by how much remains beyond my grasp.

This experience isn't about uncovering her past—it's about challenging the beliefs I've held onto for so long. It's about understanding that the narratives we create to protect ourselves can sometimes become cages that trap us. I'm beginning to recognize that knowing my mother might mean letting go of the deceptive beliefs I've relied on.

One recurring thought is about legacy—not in terms of possessions but in the emotional and psychological patterns we inherit and pass down. What traits and behaviors have I absorbed from her unknowingly? Is there a part of her that lives in me, how I react, my fears, and how I approach life? And if so, which aspects do I want to embrace, and which ones must I release to become my person truly?

I'm also noticing the subtle ways her absence has shaped me, just as much as her presence might have. The gaps she left in my life have had their defining influence, a paradox I hadn't fully grasped before—that the empty spaces, the missing pieces, hold their kind of power.

As I think about my role as a parent, it becomes clear that coming here seeking insight into my upbringing has led me to examine how I'm shaping my daughter's life. How will she perceive my choices and the reasons behind them? This awareness is unsettling because it shows me that the concerns we wrestle with don't end with us—they carry forward, shaping the future in ways we can guide but never fully control.

Chapter 21: Veil of Returning Secrets

The past has a way of catching up with you, no matter how far you go or how much you try to hide it. On my way back to Yaoundé, I longed for home. The streets, the faces of loved ones, and routine couldn't cover what lay beneath.

There was a tension I couldn't quite name, as if the city knew about the secrets I was close to uncovering. While preparing for what was ahead, something was building that would make me face truths I wasn't ready for. It wasn't just the memories but the ones I hadn't buried deep enough. They were rising, ready to break through.

I was being drawn toward something inevitable. This wasn't an ordinary return—it was a journey into the unknown, where each step forward took me deeper into something I couldn't yet understand.

This chapter shows the strength of facing the unknown, where the past and present meet and the way forward is unclear. It's a story of hesitation, persistence, and the will to face what lies within and beyond. Despite the uncertainty, I was ready to move forward, my spirit steady.

****

The bus from Yokadouma rattled along the road, carrying the smells of sweat and food. I held my daughter close, her breath barely noticeable against the vibrations and the voices around us. So much has changed since I last took this road. Back then, she was hidden inside me, a secret. Now, she was here, a reminder of how life had altered, and I was going home, facing new realities.

The bus continued, and my thoughts drifted to my grandmother, half-siblings, and Bernard, who had become necessary to us. But Elso, Amina's father, stayed in my mind. His voice, once clear, had faded. His calls were fewer, and each one felt empty, as if our bond was loosening. I couldn't explain why, but the loss was hard to ignore.

We neared Yaoundé, and I thought about the future. I had left with questions, but now I was returning, determined to build a life for my daughter and myself. It wouldn't be easy, but I was ready and focused on creating a life where the past wouldn't control our future.

When the bus stopped at the station, I felt many emotions. The city's noise surrounded me, but my mind was on seeing Elso. I stepped off the bus, holding Amina, and dialed his number.

"Elso, I'm here. I have our baby with me."

There was a pause before he answered, his voice hard to read. "I'll be there soon."

Time passed slowly as I stood in the crowd, waiting. When Elso arrived, his eyes went straight to her. Without a word, he came closer, his face softening as he reached out. "May I hold her?"

I placed her in his arms. Something shifted in him at that moment—an emotion I hadn't seen before.

He looked at her, silent for a while, then spoke, and everything around us faded.

"Hello, Amina," he said. "I'm your papa. I've waited to meet you, and now that you're here, I can hardly believe it. You look just like your mother. I'm sorry it took me so long to see you, but I'm here now, and I want you to know that I'll always be here for you. You'll grow strong, and I'll do my best to be the father you need."

Amina stirred slightly. Elso smiled and continued, "There's so much I want to teach you and show you. But for now, just know that you are mine."

He held her closer, resting his cheek against her head, trying to remember the moment. It was just the three of us, standing in the station, connected in a way words couldn't capture.

I asked, "How have you been?"

Elso looked up, calm but distant. "I'm doing well," he said.

I hesitated, unsure how to close the gap between us. "I was thinking of visiting you in a couple of days. I want to share more about my time in Yokadouma."

His answer surprised me. "It might be better if you wait until the end of the month," he said, his tone measured. "By then, I'll have enough saved for you and the baby."

I assented, processing his words. Something in his voice disguised deeper concerns, but I decided not to press further. "Okay," I agreed. "I'll wait until the end of the month."

His response troubled me, and I signaled agreement, my mind spiraling. Was it the pressure of his job as a merchant, constantly dealing with demanding customers, which made him so distant? Or was it the weight of his religious commitments— daily prayers and faith expectations? With Ramadan approaching, the fasting was already taking its toll, leaving him exhausted and withdrawn.

Yet, something else lingered. There was friction in his voice, a vacillation that didn't fit the reasons I was considering. But I didn't suspect there might be more stress from his family, arrangements being made in my absence, and a potential spouse he was encouraged to meet. These thoughts never crossed my mind then, but they would come to light later, untangling pieces of a story I hadn't known I was part of.

For now, I chose to respect his wishes and wait until the end of the month to see him again.

After that unnerving conversation, I returned home, where my thoughts were briefly interrupted by the warmth of my family's welcome. The door swung open, and I stepped forward with excitement.

My grandmother stood, her eyes brimming, a look that spoke of countless prayers answered. Without hesitation, she embraced me, wrapping her arms around me. She reassured me that I was home now and safe, no matter what happened or lay ahead.

Quick footsteps filled the hallway. Before I knew it, my half-siblings were there, their faces alight with joy. Laughter spread through the house, breaking the silence that had defined my days in Yokadouma.

At that moment, the house transformed into a refuge where I could release the tension that had gripped me for so long. I felt the glow of their welcome settle deep within me, a reminder that this was where I fit in. For the first time in what felt like ages, I allowed myself to relax, knowing I was with those who mattered most.

But that peace was short-lived. It was the end of the month, and I was on my way to meet Elso again. The closer I got to his place, the more unease settled in my stomach. When I arrived, it was clear I had been expected, though in an unusual way.

Fatimatou, Elso's mother, approached with deliberate steps, and there was a narrow space between us. I hadn't met her before, but I knew of her. Elso had shown me a photograph once, a snapshot of his family. He had often spoken of her, describing her as reserved, possessing strength that now felt unnervingly detached in this encounter.

Her face was a mask of calm, but beneath that facade, I felt something foreboding that made my skin crawl. "I've been waiting for you," she said. "I almost thought you wouldn't come, but Elso confirmed you were on your way."

A wave of confusion and dread surged within, tightening around my chest. My voice trembled. "Why were you waiting for me?"

Her eyes flickered away, avoiding my gaze. When she spoke, her words were vague, almost evasive, laced with a casualness that felt wrong. "There's a package inside for you," she said. You should go in and get it."

Her unwillingness to enter the apartment only deepened the dread curling in my stomach. I swallowed hard and moved around her, the cold grip of fear tightening. My hand shook when I reached for the door, the knock loud in the stillness, each creak reverberating through the silence like a death knell.

As I crossed the threshold, breathing became difficult. The door clicked shut behind me, sealing me in a suffocating silence as though the walls were closing in.

I took a few hesitant steps forward, my pulse pounding in my ears. The sight that met me felt like a blow to the chest, leaving me reeling. The apartment was warm, but the essence of our shared moments had disappeared. Every trace of Elso, every piece of our life together, had been wiped clean as though none had ever existed.

But aside from the emptiness, something stood out—a large brown box sat in the center of the living room, its presence sinister. On top of it was a white envelope against the dull cardboard, waiting to reveal whatever truth had been left behind. The bedroom, too, was vacant—everything was gone except for that solitary box.

Panic gripped me as I darted around the room, searching desperately for some explanation, some clue that might make sense of this sudden erasure of our lives. But there was nothing. Once witnesses to our laughter and whispered moments, the walls loomed over me like silent, indifferent sentinels.

I stood still as time stretched. Tears welled up, and before I knew it, I was sobbing. I couldn't bring myself to approach the box or reach for the envelope. The dread of what it might hold paralyzed me.

It felt like hours had passed. I paused, afraid and utterly alone in that space. An hour, maybe more, had slipped away since I first stepped inside, though it could have been mere minutes for all I knew. Fatimatou remained outside, a ghostly presence that haunted the periphery of my awareness, her purpose inscrutable, like the box's contents, which now held all my fears.

She stepped back inside and must have sensed my paralysis and the panic that had seized me. After a long time, she entered, her presence breaking the thick calm. Her eyes moved to the bin, then back to me, with a flash of pity or understanding.

"Do you need help getting it outside?" she asked. "I can help you put it in a taxi."

I hesitated, overwhelmed, but knew I couldn't manage alone. "Yes," I replied.

She moved to the box without another word, lifting one end while I took the other. Together, we carried it out of the apartment. The trip down the stairs felt like a descent into the unknown. The taxi was waiting at the curb, its engine running. With Fatimatou's help, we loaded the box into the trunk, and she closed it.

I climbed into the taxi, my head spinning. As we drove away, I watched the apartment fade, the box and envelope still untouched. The ride was a blur; I couldn't process what had happened.

When I arrived home, the house greeted me, but it did little to calm the turmoil inside. I carried the box to my room; its weight felt heavy. My grandmother and half-siblings were waiting for me, but I couldn't face them.

"I need some space," I said quietly, avoiding their eyes. "I need to rest. Could you take care of Amina for a while?"

They nodded. My grandmother took Amina's diaper bag and left the room.

I was alone and couldn't open the box or face whatever truth was inside. I lay down, sank into the mattress, stared at the ceiling, and fell asleep.

When I woke up the next day, sunlight filtered through the curtains, warming the room. I heard faint sounds of laughter from the living room. I noticed my grandmother playing with Amina. She looked up and smiled when she saw me.

"Good morning. Are you alright? I knocked on your door last night to wake you for dinner, but you were asleep," she said, her voice showing concern.

I forced a smile, trying to hide my inner turmoil. "I'm fine, grandma."

Rose and Babou had gone to school, and my grandmother was preparing to head to the farm. I knew what needed to be done, but it felt overwhelming. I needed support.

I called Amandine, my closest friend. "Can you come over? I need you here. I can't handle this alone,"

Amandine agreed without hesitation. "Of course, I'll be right there."

There was shared agitation and an unspoken understanding of the situation when she arrived. She was ready but just as apprehensive. We walked to my room. Amina sat contentedly on the bed, unaware of the disturbance.

Amandine knelt by the box and began peeling away the tape. Her hands were steady, but her eyes showed stress.

"Hey, it's going to be alright," Amandine said, meeting my gaze. "No matter what's in there, we'll face it together."

I agreed, but fear of what I might find inside lingered. Amandine's presence was my only anchor.

With a final pull, the tape came off. I reached for the lid, knowing I couldn't turn back. We prepared to discover the contents together, bracing ourselves for the unknown.

Reflection

Laying there, staring at the ceiling, I felt everything that had happened, and they began to burden me. It wasn't about the tub sitting threateningly in the corner of the room or the folder that held who-knows-what revelations. It was about my choices, my routes, and the consequences unfolding before me. Life has a way of defying us with our retrospective, no matter how much we try to outrun it, and in these moments of insight, we are forced to face the truth of who we are and what we've become.

I found myself contemplating the choices that brought me to this point. What was once insignificant is now something almost unrecognizable. How often do we need to understand their impact fully? How frequently do we step through doors, unaware of the worlds and lives we are altering? Our ways shape our future we may not always foresee.

It's easy to get caught up in the momentum of life, to let one day blur into the next, and to forget that each moment is a thread in the wave of our existence. But what happens when we finally stop and look at that design? What stories are woven into its canvas? What regrets? What triumphs? And most importantly, what veracities are hidden in our created patterns?

Think about the choices made—the small, the big, and all those in between. How have they shaped your life? How have they styled the lives of those around us? Are there things left unresolved, mysteries buried, or sincerity avoided? What would happen if they were finally faced? Would we be ready?

The antecedent is never really gone; it's always with us, just waiting for the right moment to reappear. It can seep into the current, influencing decisions, sentiments, and relationships we don't always see until it's too late. It's in the choices not made, the unsaid words, and the passageways not taken. And it's in the memories that refuse to fade, no matter how much we try to forget.

I prepared to open the box and understood I was not just opposing its contents but also addressing parts of myself that I'd kept out of sight. I'm trepidatious about what I might find—whether it offers closure or reopens old wounds. Will it give answers or lead to more uncertainties? Most importantly, will it provide choices? How do I perceive myself and my choices?

What enigmas are kept—from others and even from oneself? What facts are we afraid to disclose? And what would happen if we finally did? The answers may not be easy, but they are necessary, for it is only by facing our past that we can understand our present and shape our future.

Chapter 22: Unspoken Words.

After making a choice, there's a moment when its impact starts to appear. This was one of those times. Moving from doubt to action isn't easy; it involves steps, each bringing something new. At the start of this phase, it was clear that what we do now shapes what happens next. With that, I focused and moved forward, ready for what lay ahead.

****

Amandine handed me the envelope from the top before we opened the lid. It was creased, having been opened and closed many times. I set it aside and braced myself as we started to uncover the items inside.

My belongings, including shoes, clothes, and the outfit Elso had chosen for Amina and me, were neatly packed. There were also artworks I had sent him, along with letters and poetry. Hidden among them was about 300,000 Cameroonian CFA ($500)—a sum that felt significant and meaningless at that moment.

I hesitated before opening the envelope. Inside was a letter that made the situation real. Elso wrote that by the time I read it, he would be far away, settling in the United States. He explained that leaving without saying goodbye was the only way he could cope, and admitted that facing Amina and me was too much for him. He promised to send money and reach out once settled, but his words felt empty.

His letter stirred memories of my mother's struggle after my father left for Nigeria when I was just a baby. Now, I found myself in a similar situation, dealing with the pain of abandonment. It felt like history was repeating itself, and I couldn't stop it.

I began to wonder if this was something deeper in our culture. Did men believe it was acceptable to walk away from their responsibilities? My father had left without looking back, and now Elso was doing the same. This seemed like more than personal failures—a pattern that made me question my relationships, identity, and place within this culture. I was left in deep reflection, trying to understand my emotions and the cultural impact.

Douala stayed in my mind, driving me to uncover the truth. My mother once told me that I had to return to where it all began to find my father. The thought made my heart race, though I barely remembered the place. I had left when I was just a year old, but I knew it had the needed answers.

When I arrived, I stood outside the home of Samuel, a neighbor my mother had mentioned. He knew who I was right away. After I explained why I had come, he didn't hesitate. He called his daughter, Alice, and asked her to take me to my aunt Ndenge's house, where I might find more answers.

We arrived at my aunt's house, and the door opened, revealing a surprised and emotional woman. She recognized me immediately and began to cry, telling me how much I resembled my father. Holding Amina, I felt a surge of hope. I was finally going to get the answers I had been seeking.

Inside, the house exceeded my expectations—far more than the modest setting I had imagined. My aunt's home reflected her success, but I stayed focused on finding any sign of my father. I scanned the walls, searching for a photograph, a keepsake—anything that might connect me to him.

After an endless polite conversation, I couldn't hold back anymore. "Where is he?" I asked.

"He's not here," my aunt said, her voice calm but firm. My heart sank.

"Is he dead?" I asked, dreading the answer.

"No, no," she quickly reassured me. "He lives in Belgium. He calls me occasionally. When he does, I'll let him know you were here."

Knowing he was alive but far away left me feeling both relieved and frustrated. I pressed for more. "Will he call today?"

"No," she said, "he calls randomly."

I gave her my phone number, expecting to hear from him one day. She invited me to stay for dinner, but I declined. The information wasn't enough to keep me there. I needed time to process these new discoveries.

With a photograph of my father in hand, I felt something stir inside. I now knew his name, had seen his face, and held onto a small part of his life. But the path to truly knowing him and understanding the cultural patterns was far from complete.

Returning to school wasn't just about education but about reclaiming control of my future. With Mr. Bernard's help, I re-enrolled in high school, determined to finish what I had started.

The routine of classes, homework, and exams became a welcome break from the struggles that had defined my life.

Living with my grandmother and half-siblings brought some stability, even as I juggled the challenges of being both a student and a young mother. Each day required careful balancing, but having direction felt right. Slowly, I began to shed the protective shell I had built around myself, imagining a future shaped by my own choices, not the actions of others.

Just as I was settling into this new phase, something unexpected happened.

It was a quiet evening, six to ten weeks after my trip. The phone rang as I sat, helping Amina with her toys. I answered, thinking it was another routine call. But the voice on the other end made my heart skip.

"Hello," the voice said, hesitant, unfamiliar yet somehow known.

"Hello," I replied, unsure. There was a long pause, the silence stretching endlessly.

I knew who it was, but I couldn't speak it. The word "dad" caught in my throat, refusing to come out. Saying it would make everything real—the abandonment, the lost years, the unresolved feelings simmering inside.

He spoke again, breaking the silence. "It's me, Bachot."

Hearing his name confirmed what I already knew, but it didn't make it any easier. I had pictured this conversation so many times, but now that it was real, I felt lost, unsure of what to say or how to react. "I wasn't sure if you would call me," I said.

"I wanted to," he replied, his tone soft, almost apologetic.

I hesitated, unsure how to start the conversation.

There was another pause, and I felt everything—the questions, the hurts, and the years of silence. It was too much to resolve in one conversation.

"I'm glad you did," I said, trying to keep my emotions steady. "It would be nice if you could visit. I'd like to see you."

"I'll try," he said, but there was hesitation in his voice, unsure if he could follow through. "I'll call you back."

And just like that, the conversation ended. The phone went silent, leaving me with a lot to process. Everything stirred inside, making it hard to think clearly.

I sat there for a long time, the phone still in my hand, wondering what would come next. Part of me wanted to believe this was the start of something new: we could finally build a relationship after all these years. But another part of me sensed it wouldn't be that simple.

One thing was clear—I couldn't let doubt control me. I had a life to create, a daughter to care for, and a path to follow. Whatever happened with Bachot, I was determined to keep moving step by step.

Before that call, visiting Belgium had never crossed my mind, but once the idea came up, it became all I could think about. After several brief conversations later, he suggested it might be easier if I visited him. He had a family now, and bringing them all to Yaoundé was difficult. The thought of stepping into his world was both exciting and unsettling.

Before long, we started planning my visit to Belgium. I needed to get a passport, something I had never needed before. Though the process was hard, the idea of meeting him and seeing his life kept me going. Each step brought me closer to a reality that once felt distant.

Reflection

Moving through the experiences tied to my past, I began to see things differently. The choices made by Elso and others had shaped my life, but I realized their absence couldn't dictate what came next. I had to move forward on my terms.

Visiting Belgium was about more than meeting someone from my past. It was a chance to understand the forces that had influenced my life. It meant confronting the societal and family norms that had driven decisions long ago.

I was taking control of my story by stepping into this new phase. Despite the challenges of distance and doubt, connecting with my father wasn't just about finding answers but about creating a future on my terms. Each choice became less about the past and more about shaping the life I wanted for myself and my daughter.

Chapter 23: Crossing Borders, Journey to Brussels

Going to Brussels was more than just a trip. It meant leaving behind what I knew for something different. I faced challenges like getting the proper documents and arranging care for my daughter. As Cameroon disappeared beneath the clouds, it became clear that crossing borders was not just a physical move. It was a step toward the answers I had been looking for.

****

With the plans set, I focused on what needed to be done. Though hesitant, my family agreed and supported me, knowing it was only for three weeks. Bachot sent money for the travel papers, and I picked it up from Western Union. His wife, Brigitte, who was expecting, took care of the immigration paperwork, including the affidavits to sponsor my visit to Belgium. She worked at the bank, providing the steady income needed. While waiting for her to finish, I prepared everything to apply for the visa at the embassy.

Brigitte's paperwork was crucial. Without it, nothing would move forward. Every day, I thought about how much I depended on it. The documents meant more to me than anything else—they were the key to my past. Once I had them, there would be no turning back. During this time, I ensured my daughter would be well cared for while I was away. I spoke with my family to ensure she had everything she needed. I set aside money for her care, knowing it had to be enough. Leaving her behind for a few weeks was hard but necessary. I explained everything to her, reassuring both that I would return soon. With the paperwork almost done, I began thinking about what I needed for the trip. Cameroon's climate left me with little warm clothing.

Finally, the affidavits arrived, and I scheduled an appointment at the embassy. The process was simple but stressful. My interview was set, a necessary step to get the visa. The embassy needed specific documents, including proof of my plans, financial stability, and the reason for my visit. The affidavit from Brigitte helped show my sponsorship and support. They also needed my passport, photos, and proof of health insurance, which were standard for the application. With everything in order, I prepared for the interview. A few weeks later, I got a call from the consulate. My visa for Belgium was ready for pickup. It felt unreal, but I was relieved. I went to the embassy to collect it. The trip was finally becoming real.

With the visa in hand, leaving was now certain. In the next few days, I gathered what I needed—warm clothes and essential documents. Every item I packed was a step closer to what lay ahead. The day before I left, I stayed with my daughter and family, trying to keep things regular. However, the upcoming separation was on everyone's mind. I reassured Amina, my grandmother, and my siblings that I would return soon, even as our last moments together felt more significant than usual. My grandmother's concern was evident, and Amina clung to me longer than usual.

These moments reminded me that this wasn't just about finding answers but building a future. When the day came, there was no other option but to move forward. I boarded the plane, watching everything familiar fade away. The destination was uncertain, but the journey would change everything. Arriving in Brussels felt like stepping into another world. Everything was different in the surroundings, language, and atmosphere, but instead of feeling lost, I embraced the change. This was the moment I had been preparing for. My thoughts quickly turned to what was next and what I might discover.

<u>Reflection</u>

This step means leaving behind the past and going to a different place. The process wasn't easy, but it was needed. Each part of the trip, from saying goodbye to arriving in Brussels, showed how I was moving ahead in life.

Chapter 24: Arriving in Brussels and Discovering Belgium

The captain's voice came over the intercom, explaining the landing process. My heart raced as I looked out the window at the city below. The plane dipped and turned. This was my first flight, and it was the moment I would meet my father.

As the plane touched down, I gripped the armrest, feeling the wheels hit the runway. Everything felt authentic and new. My mind raced. What would my father be like? What about his wife, Brigitte, and the kids? I had no idea what to expect.

When the plane stopped, I followed the other passengers out. The airport was full of people rushing around, speaking languages I could sometimes understand. It felt overwhelming, but I kept moving, trying to stay calm.

As I walked into the terminal, I saw them. My father held a sign with my name. Next to him stood a woman, who I assumed was Brigitte, and two girls, Dorah and Jaelle. This was my family in Belgium.

I approached them, and my father's face lit up when he saw me. There was a calm, friendly look in his eyes. "Cara," he said, pulling me into a hug. Hugging someone I had never met but always knew about felt strange.

"Hi," I managed, trying to smile. Brigitte stood beside him, holding a baby, Corentin. "Welcome," she said softly, as if she didn't want to overwhelm me. "Thanks," I replied, glancing at the two girls beside her. They gave me small smiles and waves.

We collected my luggage and walked out of the airport together. The air outside was cool and different from Cameroon's. As we headed to the car, I noticed how everything seemed larger than I was used to. I had only been here for a few weeks, but it already felt like I had entered a different world.

Outside, we reached a parking lot. There was an older BMW from the 1990s, which seemed to have its own stories. My father opened the trunk and carefully placed my luggage inside. I took in everything around me—the lights, the streets, the buildings.

Once we were all in the car, I expected we'd go straight home after the long journey. I was tired and ready to settle in, but instead, we stopped at a store to get some toiletries for me. It struck me as odd, almost frustrating. After traveling for hours, this was the last thing I wanted. I couldn't figure out why I needed things to be taken care of before I arrived. This slight detour felt unnecessary, but I tried to adjust, even though my frustration was quietly building.

We walked into the store, and I followed behind, feeling a little out of place. The shelves were lined with colorful items, and the girls ran ahead, excited. I watched them, wondering what role I'd play in their lives. Would they like me? Would I fit in here?

After picking up what I needed, we went to the counter, got charged, and headed out. We returned to the car, ready to go to my father's home.

We continued driving through the city until we finally arrived at his place. It was a traditional building in Brussels with three bedrooms and two baths in an area called La Basilique. The buildings were tall, just as I had imagined.

Inside, the place was simple—just a home. We didn't talk much as we settled in. I was trying to process everything, trying to stay calm.

Dinner brought its challenges. I noticed him watching me closely as I ate, and then he asked if I always ate with my hands. The question stung. He tried to show me how to use a fork and spoon. The frustration I had been holding onto all day started to build. It wasn't just about the way I ate—it was about how everything felt off since I arrived. I had expected things to be different, but not in this way. It felt like he was more interested in correcting me than getting to know me.

After dinner, I went to my room, hoping for peace, but he called me out again before I could get comfortable. He wanted to talk, to learn more about me. As we sat down, I noticed he had a recorder. He wanted to record everything I said, making me even more uneasy. Why was he recording me? I didn't understand. The frustration grew as I began sharing my story—about my childhood, the struggles I faced, and the things my grandmother had told me. I needed to know if what she said was true. As I spoke, I watched him for any reaction, anything to show he was moved. But there was nothing. He listened, but it felt like he wasn't there with me.

What made it worse was that his family was also listening. This was supposed to be a conversation between us, but it felt like my story wasn't mine anymore. I felt even more alone.

Eventually, I told him I was tired. He paused the recording machine, kissed me goodnight, and I went to sleep, feeling drained and more confused than ever.

Day 2:

Morning came, and I got up quietly. The apartment was already busy with the sounds of the day starting. Bachot greeted me and said we were going out for pastries. His tone was calm, as if he was trying to start fresh.

I wasn't sure what to expect from today. We left and walked through the street. The pastry shop was about three miles away near Basilique.

The walk was long, giving me time to think. It felt like I was trying to understand the man beside me, figuring out how to connect with him. When we reached the shop, the smell of fresh bread was tempting. We chose a few pastries and sat down to eat. It was a quiet moment, but felt like a small step toward something better. I wanted to make the most of it, even though I wasn't sure what that meant.

We sat at a table, and I tried to find the right words to start a conversation. The quiet between us wasn't uncomfortable, but I could sense we were both trying to figure out this new dynamic—strangers trying to be more. After a few moments, Bachot asked how I was finding Brussels. It was a simple question, but opened the door to something more profound.

"It's different," I said. "Everything is new—the buildings, the streets, even how people talk. It's a lot to take in."

He understood but didn't push. I appreciated that he gave me space to adjust. As we continued talking, the conversation drifted to deeper topics. He told me about the neighborhood, the Christian community, and how he'd been coming here for years. For a moment, I could see him as just a regular guy, not the father I had been estranged from for so long.

When we finished at the shop, we started walking back home. The streets were getting busier. I watched the people, wondering how different or similar their lives might be to mine. Bachot suggested we visit some nearby sites, like Park du Cinquantenaire and Park de Bruxelles. I agreed, thinking that seeing more of the city might help ease the awkwardness between us.

When we returned to his place, the rest of the family was already up. The noise of daily life replaced the quiet of the morning, and I found myself retreating, unsure how to fit in. Brigitte was busy in the kitchen with breakfast, Dorah and Jaelle were playing, and baby Corentin was in his crib. Brigitte greeted us with a smile and asked how our morning was. I gave a polite answer, but I still felt out of place.

Dorah and Jaelle were shy but curious. They asked me simple questions—where I was from and what I liked to do. I answered, trying to connect, but I could tell they weren't sure how to fit me into their lives.

The morning went on, and Brigitte suggested we all sit together for breakfast. We gathered around the table, and I tried to join the conversation. It was mostly small talk—how they spent their weekend, what the girls were learning in school, and plans for the day. I listened more than I spoke, still feeling like an outsider.

Day 3:

The morning started like the day before. I woke up early, unsure of what the day would bring. I'd spend time with

Brigitte, just the two of us today. It was a chance to get to know her better, away from the family.

Brigitte was already up, getting ready for the day. I watched her move efficiently, preparing to take the kids to school and daycare. After breakfast, we loaded the kids into the car. Dorah and Jaelle seemed excited, chatting about their day. After dropping them off, Brigitte and I headed into the city.

We went to a shopping district in the heart of Brussels. The streets were busy with shops and cafes. We browsed through boutiques, and Brigitte moved confidently, engaging with other shoppers. As we moved from store to store, she shared more about her life—her early days in Brussels, meeting Bachot, and raising their children. I listened, taking in the details she shared. Her words made me feel included.

We stopped for lunch at a small café Brigitte liked. It was intimate, with tablecloths and the smell of fresh coffee. We ordered sandwiches and sat by the window, watching the world go by. During lunch, Brigitte asked me about my life in Cameroon. I found myself sharing more than I had planned—

stories from my childhood and the challenges I'd faced. She listened closely, her attention fully on my words.

The rest of the afternoon passed as we continued shopping. It was a comforting day, full of exchanges and sharing moments. When we returned to the apartment, I felt like the day with Brigitte had been a step forward in finding my place here.

That evening, we gathered for dinner as a family. The meal was calm, the conversation flowed naturally, and I joined in more. The tension I'd felt before seemed to have lifted, replaced by a new understanding.

After dinner, I returned to my room, reflecting on the day. It had been a good day—marked by small but meaningful steps.

The Weekend:

My first week in Brussels was full of new experiences and emotions. As the weekend approached, Bachot and Brigitte suggested we visit La Grande Place, one of the most famous landmarks in Belgium. They wanted me to see it and feel the heart of the city. We set out in the late afternoon, just as the sun began to dip.

The atmosphere differed from earlier in the week—excitement and a sense that something special awaited us. I was struck by its beauty and grandeur as we approached La Grande Place. Ornate buildings, rich with history and intricate detail, surrounded the square. The polished stone streets and architecture were unlike anything I had seen before. This was the heart of Belgium, and I could feel its pulse in every corner.

We wandered through the square, taking in the sights. The buildings were lit, adding a magical touch to the place. People, both locals and tourists, filled the square, all drawn to this iconic part of the city. I could see why it was so beloved and important.

For dinner, we chose an Italian restaurant called La Piola. The food was incredible, and the conversation was light and enjoyable. As I watched people move through the square, I admired how they belonged there. For the first time all week, I felt a connection to the city. With its history and beauty, this place made me feel like I was becoming part of something larger.

After dinner, we stopped by Chocolatier Elisabeth to pick up some chocolates, and I couldn't resist bringing some home.

We also grabbed waffles from a street vendor—a treat I had been eager to try since arriving in Belgium. We walked through the square one last time before heading back.

As we walked, I wanted to hold on to the moment, knowing it would stay with me long after I left Belgium. That weekend, La Grande Place became the highlight of my first week in Brussels. It was more than just visiting a landmark—it felt like a step forward.

We headed back to the apartment, and for the first time, I felt like I was beginning to find my footing.

Although the experience had its conflicts and pain, there were also moments of beauty I could carry. I knew the lessons I learned in Belgium would stay with me.

Chapter 25: Final Journey in Belgium

The weekend at La Grande Place had left me feeling more connected to Brussels, but as Monday rolled around, I knew there was still much to discover. Week two was starting, and with it came the chance to explore this new life. Monday started. The city outside was coming to life, and I was finding ease in the routines of the house. Brigitte was up when I stepped out of my room to make breakfast. Dorah and Jaelle were getting ready for school, and the excitement from the weekend was still present.

I joined them at the table, more at ease than I had been the week before. The initial awkwardness was fading, replaced by familiarity. Breakfast was casual, and the conversation focused on the plans for the day. Bachot mentioned he had work, and Brigitte had errands to run. I decided to spend the day exploring more of the city alone. After the morning bustle, the apartment grew calm. I took my time getting ready, thinking about where to go.

Brussels has much to offer, and I wanted to take it all in at my own pace. I decided to visit the Royal Grand Houses of Laken, a place I had heard about and was curious to see. The Grand House was a vast marble structure with exotic plants worldwide.

As I walked through the glass corridors, I felt peaceful. The beauty of the place was overwhelming, but in a way that calmed the soul. I wandered through the sections, breathing in the fresh floral air. It was a place where I could lose myself in thought, where the world's worries felt distant. After the morning at the

Grand House, I explored more of the city. I wandered through the streets, stopping at small cafes and shops, taking in the everyday life of Brussels.

Understanding the languages around me—French, English, and bits of Dutch and Flemish—helped me feel more connected to the city. I could follow conversations, engage with locals, and find my way around. The more I walked, the more I felt like a part of Brussels. It was during one of these walks that I met Stéphane. I had stopped at a small bookshop near Place Sainte-Catherine, drawn in by the inviting atmosphere and the promise of a good book.

As I browsed the shelves, Stéphane started a conversation. He was friendly and curious, asking about the book I was holding and what brought me to Brussels. We talked for a while, realizing we both loved literature and were curious about the world. Stéphane had traveled a lot and had a way of making the city come alive through his stories. He offered to show me around, taking me to places outside the usual tourist spots. I hesitated at first, but his easygoing nature put me at ease.

Over the next few days, Stéphane became my guide, showing me parts of Brussels I might not have found alone. We visited local markets, hidden cafes, and lesser-known landmarks, offering a fresh city view. His knowledge and excitement made me feel like an adventurer. Feeling comfortable with our friendship, I considered inviting Stéphane to my father's home. I casually mentioned him to my dad, not expecting much reaction.

To my surprise, my dad seemed agreeable, so I extended the invitation. It felt like a step forward, bringing a new friendship into this complex family dynamic. When Stéphane arrived, we settled in the living room, jabbering like before. The conversation flowed naturally, and I felt relaxed and happy to have a part of my new life in Brussels that blended with my family life. But as we talked, I noticed something off. My younger sister, Jaelle, kept hovering nearby, pretending to be occupied but clearly watching us. It felt strange, but I tried to brush it off.

Not wanting to ruin the evening, I didn't realize my father had instructed Jaelle to spy on us and report what was happening. As Stéphane and I continued our conversation, I had no idea about the watchful eyes behind the scenes. Later that evening, after he left, the atmosphere in the house changed. My father called me into the living room, his face serious. I sensed something was wrong, but I didn't know what. Then, in a harsh tone, he accused me. He demanded to know if anything inappropriate had happened—if we kissed, if there had been anything more. Shocked, I tried to explain that we had only been talking, nothing else. But my words didn't seem to matter. His anger grew, and his accusations cut deep. He called me names and humiliating words, accusing me of disrespecting him and the family.

As he spoke, I felt the weight of cultural expectations. In his eyes, I had crossed a line I didn't even know existed. The gap between how I saw things and how he did seemed impossible to bridge. Stéphane had been respectful, but here I was, facing anger that felt disconnected from the truth.

No matter how much I tried to explain, he wouldn't listen. The image in his mind, shaped by Jaelle's story, was fixed, and nothing I said could change it. By the end of the conversation, he made it clear: Stéphane was no longer welcome. I wasn't allowed to invite him over again. That night, I retreated to my room, deeply upset. The friendship that had brightened my week felt shattered by misunderstanding and misplaced anger.

The hurtful words had already sunk deep, leaving a wound that couldn't heal quickly. Listening to the argument, I was grateful that Brigitte stood up for me, trying to make him see reason. However, I also felt a growing detachment. As the voices faded and the apartment quieted, I returned to bed. I knew then the third week couldn't pass quickly enough. I was ready to go back to Cameroon.

I was still in week two, but my heart was halfway back to Cameroon. The final days in Belgium approached, and it was time to prepare for my departure. The apartment was calm, almost quiet, as everyone knew this was coming to an end. In those last days, my father tried to be more present. There were small moments—breakfasts shared, walks, conversations—touching on things we hadn't discussed before. It wasn't perfect, but it was something, and I appreciated the effort. Brigitte remained positive, encouraging our talks and ensuring everything was going as planned. As the day of my departure neared, I found myself reflecting on my time in Belgium.

It had been a journey with highs and lows, joy and frustration, and strange feelings. We both knew this was our chance to say what we needed.

"I'm glad you came, Cara," he said quietly. I looked at him, seeing the sincerity in his eyes.

I replied, "I will," and I meant it. Despite everything, there had been good moments, and I knew I would carry those with me.

The night before I was to leave, we shared a final conversation. After that, he invited me to see him play. It felt like an attempt to make amends after the difficult times, likely encouraged by Brigitte.

That night, I wore a gown given to me by Brigitte, and he dressed in a tuxedo. I was stepping into his world, and it felt like something new for a moment. The hotel where he performed was elegant, with guests dressed for the occasion. I sat at a table with food and drink, watching him at the piano.

As his hands moved over the keys, I saw him differently focused and absorbed in his music. He seemed at peace, and I saw him as fully engaged in what he loved, not the man I had struggled with. It was a side of him I hadn't known, and in that moment, the tension between us faded. The music expressed what words couldn't, and I realized there was more to him than I had understood.

After the concert, we left the hotel around 2 a.m. and returned home. I fell into bed, happy, knowing I had glimpsed a part of his life I hadn't seen before.

The following day, Brigitte helped me with my bags as I prepared to leave. Dorah and Jaelle then gave me small gifts and carefully prepared drawings.

On the way to the airport, I enjoyed the view and the scenery. I was excited about taking it all in and saving it in my memory for years. The goodbyes were short but meaningful.

My father's embrace was tighter than when I first arrived, and it was as if he was holding on to our progress. Brigitte's smile was warm. I knew she had been the bridge between us, the one who had kept things together when they could have easily fallen apart.

As I boarded the plane, I looked at the airport, the plane, and everything around me. The experience in Belgium had changed me in ways I hadn't expected. I knew I would face challenges ahead, but I had also found strength within myself that I hadn't known was there.

On the plane, I watched some TV, had dinner, and then drifted off to sleep, looking forward to waking up in Yaoundé, Cameroon.

Chapter 26: An Empty Homecoming

The plane touched down in Yaoundé, but something felt different. Walking through the gate, I expected someone to be waiting. Memories of my family gathered at the airport when I left for Belgium were still fresh. I had imagined the same welcome—hugs, smiles, and questions about my trip. But looking around, no one was there.

The absence of my family hit me harder than I thought. There had been a big send-off when I left, as if they expected something more permanent. Maybe some thought I would stay in Belgium and become their connection to a new life overseas, but now I was alone with no one to meet.

****

I gathered my luggage and pushed through the crowd. I had to find a taxi and return to Ékounou alone. The ride felt longer than I remembered, my thoughts bouncing between frustration and confusion. How could no one be there to greet me? I had been gone but not forgotten—or so I thought. The absence at the airport left an ache, a feeling I couldn't shake, as if something essential had been left behind.

When I arrived home, my grandmother was there with Rose and Babou. Their faces lit up when they saw me, which eased some of the sadness. Amina rushed into my arms, her smile reminding me why coming back mattered. Rose and Babou followed closely behind, full of energy and questions. It wasn't the homecoming I had expected, but the long trip was worth it.

As I put my things in my room and started unpacking, the disappointment from earlier stayed with me. After a shower, I sat with my grandmother, Rose, Babou, and Amina, and we shared stories. I told them about my time in Brussels, meeting Bachot, his wife Brigitte, and their children, Jaelle, Dorah, and Babou. They listened closely, asking questions about what it was like there and the people I had met.

I described Brussels in detail—the streets, the buildings towering with ornate architecture, and the cobblestone alleys that seemed to wind endlessly. The weather was cool, with a chill in the air even in the summer months, and the people moved with a hurried pace, dressed in dark coats despite the sun. The airport was alive with colors—bright reds and blues from shop signs. I talked about the food, too—the sweet and soft waffles, the smell of fresh bread, and the chocolate shops that tempted every traveler. They were curious about everything, and I found myself reliving the experience as I shared these stories. Rose and Babou asked more questions about the new family I had seen while Amina listened quietly, absorbing every word. We stayed up until it was time to go to bed, and though I still felt the earlier sadness, I was grateful for the time together.

The following day, I woke up to my old life, slipping back into the routine I had left behind. The day passed with tasks—cleaning my clothes, organizing, and being with Amina. She stayed close by my side as I sorted through everything. After a while, I shared the gifts I brought back from Belgium. Amina's eyes lit up as I handed her a small package of toys, books, and clothing. Babou and Rose were just as excited to see what I had brought for them—clothing, perfumes, and souvenirs from La Grande Place. My grandmother smiled, enjoying the postcards and smelling the bills and coins I brought for her from Belgium.

In the afternoon, I went to Yaoundé Central and started exploring. I visited a few colleges and spoke with people I knew, trying to better understand my options. I wanted to know the best direction to take—whether it was continuing with school, starting a trade, or finding training that could help me begin earning an income. When I got home, I was greeted by visitors I wasn't expecting.

Second and third cousins I had never met, whose names I didn't know, began showing up. Seeing all these people not coming to welcome me but to ask questions was overwhelming. They were more interested in knowing why I had come back, what had happened in Belgium, and why I hadn't stayed. I answered their questions and mentioned I had brought some gifts—clothes and toys for my daughter, grandmother, and half-siblings. But instead of appreciation, they laughed, made jokes, and mocked me. What I thought would be a simple gesture of sharing turned uncomfortable. They didn't just want gifts; they expected me to return with wealth, as though my time abroad should have transformed me into a provider for everyone.

That week, calls started coming from uncles on my mother's side, all wanting to know the same thing. They had heard I was back, and their questions felt endless. I didn't mention bringing any gifts for them because I could already sense the disappointment. Word spread quickly, and soon, even neighbors became involved. It felt like the whole town knew I had returned, but not in a way that felt warm or welcoming.

One afternoon, as I went to the shop to get sandwiches for Amina and myself, I could feel eyes on me. People whispered, some laughed, and I knew they were talking about me. The stares were unsettling, making me feel like an outsider like I had failed.

The disappointment was almost tangible. In Cameroon, especially as the eldest sibling, there's an expectation of success when you go abroad. Families believe that once someone leaves, they will return with wealth, ready to care for everyone. I was expected to live a lavish life, to bring money, clothes, and opportunities for the family. Returning home to the same life, with only a few gifts for my grandmother, daughter, and half-siblings, was not what they had hoped for. They expected me to elevate the entire family. Instead, I returned to where I had always been, which was unacceptable in their eyes.

When I left for Belgium, everyone was excited. There was a celebration, people cheering me on, and I hoped I would make something of myself. But now, I was the subject of their jokes. Everywhere I went, I could feel people laughing, whispering about how I had gone to Europe only to return with nothing. They'd say things like, "Look at her now, struggling. We stayed, and we're doing better than she is. What did she even achieve?"

They called me a failure, excluded me from gatherings, and clarified that I was no longer part of the group. Their excitement for me turned into disappointment—not just for them but for me. It was a lonely time, and I felt more isolated than ever.

It became impossible to leave my house. Even when I needed to go grocery shopping or run simple errands for Amina and me, I felt the stares and heard the whispers. The constant feeling that people talked about me made it too hard to be out in public. What started as quiet conversations became something sharper, more pointed. The whole situation left me feeling trapped in a place I had once called home.

Cameroon was where I had always lived, but now it felt like I didn't belong. I hadn't met their unspoken expectations—the cultural ones that said I should return successful, ready to lift everyone. But I didn't. I had nothing, and it felt like everyone turned on me because of it. I couldn't stay there anymore.

I began exploring my options, thinking through what to do next. My thoughts shifted back to Belgium, where I had at least found some stability and connection. While visiting my biological father, I met Stéphane. I started reminiscing about the long walks we shared, and the time spent at my father's home in Brussels. That life felt so different from what I was living in Cameroon. I longed for that again—a chance to explore and continue what we had started.

My grandmother was also supportive of my decision to leave. She encouraged me to seek a life where I could feel more secure and at peace, knowing I didn't have to stay where I no longer felt welcome. With her encouragement, I decided to leave, knowing it was time for a change.

After I decided to leave Cameroon, I was searching for ways to make it happen. A friend suggested something that shocked me—using dating sites to connect with people overseas. They had heard stories of others doing this, building relationships online with people abroad who helped them leave. I couldn't believe it at first. Finding someone online to help me leave felt strange, but after hearing more about these stories, I thought," Why not?" I decided to try it, though it wasn't something that immediately appealed to me.

At the time, I didn't have a computer of my own. The culture and the way I lived didn't make owning one common. So, I went to a cyber cafe where you could pay for time on the internet by the hour. You could buy thirty minutes, two hours, or even more, depending on how long you need. Sometimes, you could even reserve a specific computer if you wanted consistency. It was there that I started browsing a French dating site, but it didn't interest me much.

A week later, I returned to the cyber cafe and spent three hours exploring a dating site in Belgium, focusing specifically on Brussels. This one caught my attention. As I browsed through profiles, I eventually selected five that seemed exciting and decided to send them all initial introductions to see what would happen.

I planned to check in every two weeks. I booked the same computer at the cyber cafe and built a good relationship with the owner. That way, I could easily schedule my time for the next checkup and see if anything showed up in my inbox. It became a routine, and I stuck to it every two weeks.

When I returned to the cyber cafe, I found two emails from Wautier Guy. The first message thanked me for my thoughtful response and for providing more details about my life. The second expressed his interest in more frequent communication rather than waiting two weeks between messages, and we began talking every other day via email.

After about three months of regular emails, Guy asked if I could share my phone number. I explained that I didn't have one because they were costly in Cameroon, and I didn't have the money to afford it. That's when he offered to buy me a device so we could talk anytime, sending me three hundred euros via Western Union to help me get it.

I went to the Western Union to pick up the money and bought a Motorola cell phone with it. I still remember the color—it was yellow and black. Once I had the phone, I shared my number with Guy, and we continued our communication. It felt like a nice gesture that made me comfortable and confident about where things were headed.

As I returned to my daily routine, balancing college, caring for Amina, and spending time with my grandmother, I eagerly awaited our conversations. The excitement grew as Saturday approached.

When I checked my inbox, I found a message from Guy. He told me he would call on Saturday at six p.m. in Cameroon. The thought of hearing his voice for the first time felt almost unreal. I had seen his photos, read his emails, and pieced together an idea of who he was, but this call would bring everything to life.

Saturday felt like it couldn't come fast enough. I could hardly focus on anything else. The hours dragged on, and the closer it got to six p.m., the more my heart raced. I wondered what his voice would sound like. Would it match the person I had imagined? Would this call change everything?

As the clock ticked, I found myself pacing the room, repeatedly checking my phone. I felt excitement and nerves, each minute feeling longer than the last. I was ready to hear him.

<u>Chapter 27: The Call</u>

The day had finally come. After weeks of emails and photos, Saturday was here. I was about to hear Guy's voice for the first time. As the clock approached six p.m., I wondered what our conversation would be like. Would it feel as easy as our emails? Or would this call change everything?

This moment was more than just a phone call. It was about what might come next. Would my connection with Guy help me escape where I felt I no longer belonged? Would his voice mark the start of something new or just another chapter in my search for a better life?

****

At precisely six p.m., my phone rang. I ensured I was alone, slipping into my room and locking the door. I sat quietly, picked up the phone, and whispered, "Hello." On the other end, I heard a warm voice say, "Bonsoir, comment ça va?" His greeting in French made it real.

We talked for about two hours, covering everything from the weather to my week, day at school, family, and routine. He was curious, asking about my life and how many siblings I had. The conversation flowed naturally. His voice, photos, and emails made everything come together. For the first time, I could picture him as a complete person.

He shared about his life, his routine, and his upbringing. Gradually, we moved from emails to texts and voice calls. He frequently sent me money, around five hundred to six hundred euros a month, along with the allowance from Bernard. Things began to change for me.

Soon, word spread in town that I had met someone online, a real connection. Neighbors who had kept their distance started showing up and offering help with chores or Amina. Family members began asking questions and spending more time at my home. It was strange to see how quickly their attitudes changed.

After school, I would go home, take care of chores, help my siblings, and enjoy time with my grandmother and daughter. Every night, I made time for our calls. They became more frequent, sometimes lasting for hours until I fell asleep with the phone still in my hand. During one of these late evening calls, we decided it was time for me to meet him in Brussels.

For my second trip to Belgium, things were much easier. With my previous experience, I packed efficiently and ensured everything was in place. Before my departure, my mother came from Yokadouma, Yaoundé, to spend time with me and her granddaughter. We had a couple of weeks together, allowing us to connect and discuss the logistics of my trip. It was a short but meaningful time to get to know my mom.

We discussed my project, and I promised to call and update them once I arrived. My mom joked, "Maybe he's a serial killer," while my grandmother reassured me that everything would be fine. In the days leading up to my flight, family members traveled across Cameroon to see me off. It turned into a celebration, marking my journey back to Belgium.

My uncle, Baboulek, had been released from prison on parole and could come to the airport. We had a family dinner, followed by prayers and blessings. Three taxis were lined up: one for me, my mother, my daughter, my grandmother, and my siblings, and another for my cousins and the rest of the family. It was a big event filled with support and well-wishes.

I remember exactly what I wore: duck-sized Sebago shoes, a gray turtleneck sweater, and blue jeans. I had a bag with me, my hair was long, and I wore makeup. I felt nervous heading into the unknown again, but knowing I had already been to Belgium and had a relative there gave me confidence.

We had another round of prayers before leaving the taxi at the airport. I hugged my daughter, grandmother, mother, and siblings and waved goodbye. Entering the airport, I went through security checks, feeling strong emotions. Leaving my family was tough, but I was excited to see Guy.

After I checked in, my phone rang. It was Guy calling to make sure I was okay. He said he was ready for my arrival and would wait for me at the airport. He even sent me a photo of the outfit and car he'd be driving. His calm voice reassured me that everything would be okay. "If anything comes up, just call me," he said. I held onto my phone, comforted that I could reach him.

The flight felt endless. I was excited, anxious, and curious about what awaited me. The food came and went, but I barely noticed it. As the cabin lights dimmed, many passengers around me began to sleep. I tried to rest, but my thoughts were too active. What would it be like to meet Guy face-to-face after all our months of talking? Would our connection feel the same in person? These questions replayed in my mind as I shifted in my seat.

As the plane began its descent into Brussels, my heart raced. I rechecked my phone, re-read Guy's messages, and looked at pictures of his car. Everything felt real now, and I knew there was no turning back. This was when the future I had imagined was about to meet reality.

Walking toward the arrival gate, my eyes searched for the outfit he had described. Then I saw him wearing blue jeans and a long-sleeved cashmere shirt with matching boots near the exit. His red hair stood out, and his piercing blue eyes met mine as he saw me. He was a good-looking man, 6'2", with a sturdy build. There was warmth in his gaze that made the moment feel real. It was as if the whole world around him disappeared. Time slowed, giving me space to take in this reality.

The man who had only been a voice on the phone, a series of emails, and a few pictures was standing just a few feet away. He smiled, and at that moment, everything felt perfect. The months of waiting, the excitement, and the long hours on the phone had all led to this.

I moved forward almost automatically, closing the distance between us. Each step felt like a bridge between the life I had left behind and the one waiting for me here. When I reached him, the first word caught in my throat. "Hi." His eyes met mine, and it felt like the air held everything we hadn't yet said.

Standing in front of him felt more intense than anything I had imagined. He reached out and embraced me. The hug wasn't rushed or awkward; it was steady, firm, and familiar, as if we had been meeting like this for years. I didn't know what to say at first; it was overwhelming, but the silence felt more significant than any words. His hands rested gently on my back, and I closed my eyes for a moment, letting the moment sink in. This wasn't just the end of a journey but the beginning of something new.

Reflection

This trip to Belgium marked a turning point in my life. It wasn't just about geography; it changed how I saw myself and my future. There was uncertainty but also excitement. This journey was about embracing the unknown and trusting my instincts. Leaving behind my family and everything familiar was difficult, but moving forward meant accepting change. This was the beginning of something new, filled with possibilities.

Chapter 28: A New Beginning

Standing in the airport, the distance that had once separated us—thousands of miles, emails, phone calls—had vanished. Everything felt real. This wasn't just a trip but the start of a new chapter that could change my life.

Leaving the airport, the world around me felt fresh, opening possibilities I hadn't imagined. I had said goodbye to Cameroon, my daughter, and my family. Still, I was stepping into a different experience at that moment—one I didn't fully understand yet but was ready to explore. Walking beside him, I knew every step led me deeper into what was to come.

****

I followed him to his car, a dark sedan like the photo he had sent me. He opened the door, and I slid into the passenger seat, taking in the surroundings. The air felt fantastic. It was winter, and the sight of snow was striking. The streets were covered in snow, making everything look peaceful.

Guy's home was close to Carrefour GB, a well-known supermarket chain in Belgium. For my American readers, it's like Walmart. You can find just about anything from groceries to household goods in this large store. It was nice to know we were near such conveniences, but the best part was the neighborhood. The neighbors were friendly and respected each other's privacy. On one side lived a judge; on the other, an

English teacher and his wife worked as a personal trainer. It felt like a good place, a welcoming and secure community.

After parking, he gestured to the snow-covered garden. "In the summer, we can have barbecues by the pool," he said, smiling. It was hard to imagine the garden green and alive under the layers of snow, but the thought of staying stayed with me.

Inside, the house was even more impressive. Stepping into the living room, I saw a television, comfortable sofas, and shelves of books. The decor was modern yet inviting, with polished woodwork in a rich brown finish. The craftsmanship created a chic environment, making it feel like home. The living room led into what they called the game room, which had board games and extra seating.

Heading upstairs, I found all the bedrooms and one bathroom. The spacious attic was also upstairs and used for storage. Downstairs was another bedroom, the kitchen, and two bathrooms: one full and one half near the exit leading to the pool. It was a well-thought-out space.

The outdoor area was accessible from the ground floor, where the pool waited under its winter cover. A path led directly to Carrefour GB, a convenience I hadn't expected but appreciated. Then there was Phil, the brown Labrador. He greeted me with a wagging tail, adding to the welcoming feel of the house. Phil seemed like a gentle dog; his friendly demeanor made the home feel alive.

Before I arrived, Guy had told me about his son Vincent. He was eighteen, just like me. Knowing he had a son my age added another layer to the situation, and I looked forward to meeting him soon. After we entered the house, Guy brought in my luggage and started the tour. The house was even more impressive, and he walked me through each room. He showed me my bedroom, a separate space just for me, and mentioned I could reach out if I needed anything.

While we were touring, Vincent came out of his room, said hello briefly, and returned to his video games. Guy showed me the bathrooms and gave me a robe, saying everything was ready for my stay. My room was prepared, and the bed was made with hot pink sheets. It was sweet, especially since he had asked me about my favorite color earlier. Even though blue was my true favorite, I had chosen pink for the bedding because it represented a fairytale—a dreamlike feeling I had always held on to. Seeing the pink sheets laid out felt like a small part of that dream becoming real.

After the tour, I showered and put on the robe he had left for me. It was nice, and after the long journey, I felt relaxed and refreshed. He asked if I was hungry, but I wasn't, so we sat for a while, chatting about the trip and sharing thoughts to catch up. Before long, it was time for bed. He entered his room, and I retreated to mine, feeling calm and ready for what was ahead.

In the morning, I woke up to an amazing breakfast. The kitchen had the scents of freshly cooked omelets, French toast, coffee, russet waffles, and chocolate. It felt like a feast, almost a celebration. I hadn't expected such a grand breakfast, and the sight of all the food laid out was incredible. As we sat down to eat, the neighbors came to say hello and introduce themselves. It was a friendly welcome, and I appreciated how open everyone seemed. Conversations were light, and everyone made sure I felt at home. It was a different experience from what I had been used to, and I valued how they all made me feel included.

That evening, we went to Santorini, a well-known Greek restaurant near the Grand Place in Brussels. The Grand Place, a UNESCO World Heritage Site, is one of the most iconic landmarks in the city. Surrounded by 17th-century guild halls, the City Hall, and the King's House, its history dates back to the 12th century and has always been Brussels's cultural and political heart. We enjoyed Mediterranean dishes like gyros, souvlaki, and moussaka at the restaurant while soaking in the atmosphere with locals.

After dinner, we strolled through the Grand Place, admiring the lights and architecture. The evening felt great, as if I were experiencing another world. Before heading home, we made a quick stop at Manneken Pis, one of the city's most iconic statues. This small bronze statue of a boy urinating in a fountain has stood there since the 15th century and has become a playful symbol of Brussels. We took photos to remember the moment and continued our walk through the city.

In the following weeks, our routine settled into a rhythm. We shared meals, explored the city, and learned more about each other. One weekend, he took me to Matongé, a vibrant African neighborhood in Brussels. The restaurants and markets offered a taste of home with cuisines and products from Central, West, and North Africa. He knew I would appreciate the connection to my roots, and I did. We shared Puff-puff and Ndolé at one of the Cameroonian restaurants, and I introduced him to the flavors of my homeland. He was open to trying new things, from grilled fish to plantains and hot sauce. It felt special to share this part of myself with him in such an authentic way.

We finished the night at a local nightclub with African music that evening. Kofi Olomide's music played with its fast-paced rhythm and energy. Kofi is a celebrated Congolese musician known for pioneering the soukous dance style. His Congolese rumba and Afrobeat created a scene.

Beyond his musical talent, Kofi Olomide has made significant contributions to African culture, shaping music with his dynamic performances and leadership. He founded the band Cartier Latin International, helping to launch the careers of several well-known African artists. Listening to his music in the club brought an authentic African experience.

When we returned home that night, things felt different. I no longer slept in the space with the pink bed sheets. Instead, we shared a room. I remember waking up the next morning next to a man twenty-five years older than me. The shift in our relationship was clear. Waking up made it feel undeniable. I lay there for a moment, taking in everything. It wasn't just about the age difference; it was about how I saw myself, my perception of him, and how my world in Belgium had evolved so quickly. Part of me wondered how I had gotten there, yet another part understood that these choices had unfolded steadily, step by step. As I got up and began my morning, a new tension was in the air. It was subtle, but it was there.

He greeted me with a smile, and we continued as though nothing had changed, but things were different now. The boundary that had been there before had faded, and the lines were blurred.

Chapter 29: Defining Us

The shift from separate spaces to sharing a home marked a turning point in our relationship. A week after arriving in Belgium, we were no longer just two people living together. We were partners. Waking up next to him felt new, and we clearly needed to discuss our relationship.

"Can we talk?" I said.

"About what?" he asked.

About us. We have been sharing the same space, and things have changed. We need to figure out what this means.

"Yeah, it's important," he said.

I continued, "We can't stay silent anymore. I want to know how you see this moving forward. Are we just living together, or are we building something deeper?"

He thought for a moment. "I care about you. We should communicate more about our expectations."

We discussed our feelings and hopes, age differences, and cultural backgrounds. We hadn't agreed on everything by the end, but we decided to continue the conversation later.

After our discussion, he went to work, leaving me at home. I kept busy cleaning and organizing the house. Vincent came down to help. We chatted about school and his interests.

Later, we went to Carrefour J.B. for groceries. I got new pillows for the couch and paint for the walls. I liked having

Vincent with me. We returned home with bags of fresh food. While preparing lunch, I cooked grilled fish, plantains, and a salad. Vincent helped with the plantains. After lunch, I cleaned up and prepared dinner before Guy came home. He was happy to see everything organized.

"Looks great! When are we painting?" he asked.

"I thought we could do it this weekend," I replied.

"Perfect! I can invite some friends to help us. We'll get it done faster that way," he said.

That weekend, Guy's friends came. We chose a bright color for the living room. While we painted, Marco, one of Guy's friends, joked and pretended to spill paint on me, making everyone laugh.

Vincent helped with the roller and talked about his favorite video games. I enjoyed his energy. It felt like we were building a connection, one paint stroke at a time.

After we finished, we stepped back to admire our work. Guy's friends congratulated us, and I felt proud of what we did together.

To celebrate, Guy suggested we have a barbecue in the backyard. The weather was nice, and I loved the idea. We grilled chicken, sausages, and vegetable skewers. I made a salad to go with it.

As we gathered around the grill, I felt more at home.

I thought of my biological father. He lived in Brussels, too, and I realized he didn't know I was here. I felt excited but nervous about reaching out to him.

The next day, I called him. "Hi, it's me," I said when he answered.

"Yeah, where are you?" he asked. "I hear a different background on the phone, unlike in Cameroon. Is that a tram or a train, I hear?"

"I'm here."

"Here where?" he pressed.

"I'm in Belgium."

"Wait, what? Where in Belgium?"

"Brussels."

"No way! I watched you get on that plane! I thought you were still in Cameroon."

"I've been here for a few weeks now," I explained.

"Really? You need to give me your address," he said.

I gave it to him over the phone, and he came to visit later that week. Guy and Vincent welcomed him into our home.

"Good to see you!" I said.

"Wow, it's great to be here," he replied.

We talked, and I shared how I met Guy. "We met on a dating website. Our relationship grew. Guy wanted me to visit him in Belgium, and I agreed to come here on a visitor visa."

"That's interesting," he said. "And how's your daughter?"

"I left Amina in Cameroon with my mother and grandmother. I miss her."

He understood. "Maybe you can bring her here."

We enjoyed our time together, and when he left, he said, "Let's stay in touch. Maybe we can meet up sometime with Brigitte."

"Sounds good," I replied.

As he walked out, I thought about how much had changed. I was making connections here, but Amina was always in my mind.

A few days later, I felt unwell. At first, I thought it was just a cold. But as the days passed, I felt worse. Concerned, Guy insisted I go to the hospital.

When we arrived, the staff ran several tests. I waited, hoping for answers. Finally, the doctor came in and said I was pregnant.

I looked at Guy, and I could see he was thinking. He turned to me and said, "You're not returning to Cameroon with my baby; you will stay with me. We'll get married."

At that moment, I realized my life was changing.

As the days passed, we started planning our wedding. We wanted a simple ceremony with close people. The idea was to keep it private and intimate, followed by a small dinner. It felt right for us.

I shared the news with my father. He was concerned about me marrying at eighteen since Cameroonian law requires a person to be twenty-one. He asked if this was what I wanted, and I said yes. He knew he could not enforce the law since we were in Europe. He agreed to be my witness and walked me down the aisle.

We finalized the pre-marriage paperwork with a week left before my visitor visa expired. It was a big step, and everything felt right. My relationship with gay groups was closer, and it felt like we were building a life together.

The wedding day was joyful. My biological father and cousin, Leto, from Italy, were there, along with Guy's older brother, Leo, his son, Vincent, and our neighbor, the judge, the English teacher, and their children. Brigitte helped me get ready for the day. We got dressed and styled our hair. Surrounded by loved ones, we said wow. It was simple, but it felt special. Afterward, we celebrated with a small dinner, sharing laughter and joy.

As I looked around, I wished Amina could be there. I wanted her to be part of this new life with us.

After the wedding, I thought about Amina's situation. I wanted to bring her to Belgium, so I considered my uncle for help. I shared this with Guy, and he liked the idea. We sent money to my uncle, Baboulek, to take care of everything needed to get their passports, go to the consulate, organize interviews, obtain visas, and buy plane tickets. He was happy about the news.

Three weeks after our wedding, Amina and my uncle Baboulek arrived in Belgium. Guy and I went to Zaventem Airport to pick them up.

"Are you ready?" Guy asked as we drove.

"I can't wait to see her," I replied.

At the airport, I spotted Amina and Baboulek. She ran to me, and we hugged. "Mom!" she said, beaming.

"Thank you for bringing her, Uncle,"

We gathered our bags and headed outside. Amina looked around, taking in her new surroundings.

As we drove home, I shared stories about our life in Belgium, and she listened, excited to be part of this new chapter. Once home, I showed her around. Guy helped prepare a meal, and we sat together, exchanging joy and tales.

Amina adjusted to her new life well. I enrolled her in Pre-K, where she quickly made friends. Each day, she came home with new stories. I loved hearing about her day.

On one occasion, she excitedly told me about her new friend, Lila. "We played with blocks!" she exclaimed.

My uncle was a big help during his stay. He joined us on walks and picked Amina up from school. I noticed he sometimes looked sad, knowing he would soon return to Cameroon.

On his last day, Amina hugged him tightly. "Promise to visit again?" she asked.

"Of course," he replied. "I will always be your uncle."

After Baboulek left, I focused on my future. I went back to college to study law. While organizing the attic, I found my old phone from Cameroon. Curiosity led me to check it, and I discovered a message from Elso, Amina's dad, dated the day of my wedding. He asked what had happened and wanted me to call him immediately.

Listening to his message stirred many emotions. I hadn't heard from him in months and felt a rush of questions. I knew I needed to follow up. I dialed the number he provided, my heart racing.

As it rang, I felt anxious. This call could change everything.

After my call with Elso, I knew I had to talk to Guy about his offer for Amina to visit her father in Atlanta. That evening, I approached him.

"Can we talk about something important?" I asked.

"Sure, what's on your mind?" Guy replied.

"I just spoke with Amina's dad. He wants to see her and has offered to cover our tickets to Atlanta."

Guy's expression shifted. "How do you feel about that?"

"I think it's important for Amina to know her father. But I'm nervous about the trip. I want to make sure it's the right decision for us."

"What about Amina? Are you comfortable with the trip?"

"I am, but I want to make sure we're all on the same page," I replied. "This could change things for us."

"Let's talk to Amina together," Guy suggested. "We can explain everything and see how she feels."

Later, we sat down with Amina. "Hey, sweetie, I have something to share," I said.

"What is it, Mom?" she asked.

"Your dad wants to see you, and we might visit him in Atlanta."

Amina's face lit up. "Really? I want to see him!"

I felt relieved. Her enthusiasm was clear. "We can talk more about it, but it would mean traveling on a plane."

"Yay! I want to go!" she exclaimed.

I smiled, glad she was excited. This trip was important for her and could strengthen her bond with Elso.

Meanwhile, I wondered about Elso's situation. What had he been doing in Atlanta? Did he want to be involved in Amina's life? I hoped he had changed and would show up for her this time.

As the days passed, I continued planning. I booked the tickets and felt nervous. Guy was supportive, but I could perceive he still had reservations. We needed to keep communicating as we moved forward.

I packed our suitcases and took her favorite clothes and toys. "Do you want to bring your teddy bear?" I asked.

"Yes! Teddy has to come!" she replied.

We arrived at the airport early on the plane. Amina looked around at the busy crowd. "So many people!" she said.

Guy helped with our luggage. "Are you ready for this adventure?" he asked.

"Yes!" she shouted.

As we checked in and moved through security, I felt anxiety. Knowing this trip was important for us, I wanted everything to go smoothly.

Once on the plane, Amina settled into her seat with Teddy. The flight attendants greeted us, and I explained the journey. "We're going to see your dad," I said.

Her eyes lit up. "I can't wait!"

Amina enjoyed the snacks and the view from the window. She waved at the clouds, laughing as we flew above them. I felt relieved; she was handling everything well.

When we landed in Atlanta, the Southern sun greeted us. She looked around, eager to see her dad. As we exited the terminal, I spotted Elso waiting. He looked like I remembered. Amina rushed ahead, calling out, "Dad!"

Elso knelt to embrace her. "Amina! I've missed you!"

I watched as they connected. I approached slowly, feeling the shift in our relationship.

"Thank you for coming," I said to Elso.

"I wouldn't miss it," he replied, looking at her. "Let's make this a great visit."

The first day was just getting settled. Elso prepared a small welcome party, and I saw Amina enjoying her time with him. They played games, and he showed her around.

As the visit continued, I noticed her thriving with him. She laughed easily, and their bond seemed to grow. I felt happy for her, but the situation confused me.

That evening, after she went to bed, Elso and I talked. He wanted to reconnect romantically, trying to pull me back into our past. This changed everything, making me think about our previous relationship. He was my first love and the father of my child.

He wanted me to move to the United States. I replied, "I can't. I just applied for a new job and will start when I return to Brussels."

"What job?" he asked.

"I will be working as a paralegal for a judge. It's a step toward becoming an immigration attorney in Belgium," I explained. "I'm not interested in a life in America."

He insisted, "You should consider it."

I hesitated. "I don't want to become an illegal alien."

Elso also insisted I consider it and suggested I apply for the Diversity Visa (DV) lottery. The DV lottery is a program that allows people from eligible countries to apply for a chance to obtain a U.S. visa. A limited number of visas are available each year, and winners can live and work in the United States.

"Think about it," he urged.

This was not just about Amina seeing her dad. It involved big decisions for my future and what I wanted for us as a family.

Before we returned to Belgium, he mentioned our future living together as a family in Atlanta. "You and Amina can visit anytime," he said. He wanted to be a good father and husband.

I thought, how can he be a good husband when I'm married to someone else? I nodded, but I knew I had to be careful. Amina's happiness was my priority, but so were my feelings.

When we boarded the flight back to Brussels, I reflected on my experiences. The journey had changed me in ways I didn't fully understand. T

Then tragedy struck during the flight. I was having a miscarriage, maybe due to the stress and anxiety I felt in Atlanta. The physical pain was intense, and the emotional turmoil left me shaken. I had wanted to build a family with Guy, and now I faced the loss of our baby. This experience shattered my stability.

When we arrived in Belgium, everything felt different. I looked at Guy with confusion. I wasn't sure how to explain what had happened or how to navigate my feelings. The excitement of our life together now felt overshadowed by sadness.

I reflected on Amina's time with Elso, my feelings for Guy, and the future I envisioned for us. I needed to talk to him about everything, but the words felt difficult.

That evening, I sat down with him.

"Can we talk?" I asked.

"Of course. What's going on?" he replied, concern on his face.

I hesitated, then spoke. "I had a miscarriage on the way back from Atlanta."

His expression shifted to one of understanding. "I'm so sorry. How do you feel?"

"It's hard. I wanted to build a family with you, and now I feel lost. I don't know what this means for us," I said, tears welling up.

Guy reached for my hand. "We can get through this together."

I shook my head. "I've been thinking a lot. I want a divorce."

I could see the shock on his face. "Divorce? Why?"

"I feel confused about everything. I don't know if I can move forward with this relationship. I need time to figure out who I am and what I want," I explained.

He remained quiet for a moment, processing my words. "I didn't see this coming. I care about you, and I want to support you."

"I appreciate that, but I think it's best for both of us if we separate," I said, my voice steady.

As the conversation ended, I knew this was a difficult step, but it felt necessary for my healing and growth.

Reflection

Looking back on everything that had happened, I realized how much my life had changed. Amina's arrival brought joy, but it also came with new challenges. The trip to Atlanta opened my eyes to the complexities of family and relationships.

Elso's presence reminded me of our past and the choices I had to make. My feelings for Guy became unclear, and the loss of my pregnancy added to my confusion.

I needed to focus on Amina and what was best for her. My decision to seek a divorce was not easy, but it felt necessary. I was ready to find my path forward, whatever that may look like.

Chapter 30: New Directions

Getting to this moment had not been easy. After the challenges of my marriage and the difficulties of living in Belgium, I was ready to embrace change. With Amina by my side, I knew my decisions would shape our future. I was determined to find a path that led us to stability and happiness.

****

After I filed for divorce, the conversation with Guy turned serious. "If you don't seek any spousal support, equitable distribution of property, or support for Amina, even though she's not my biological daughter and I didn't adopt her, I will sign the divorce papers," he said. "But if you do, I won't."

"I don't want anything," I replied. It was time to make my own choices and move forward.

I called my father and said, "I'm coming to your home. I'm not with Guy anymore, and I need help." Amina and I headed to his place around midnight.

When we arrived at his home, I prepared for his reaction. He opened the door and looked at me. "This was your decision. You wanted to be married. Now, you need to figure out how to live in Belgium. Don't come back here." His words felt final. Expecting support, it became clear that navigating this path would be done alone.

Leaving his home, we walked down the dark stairs into the night. With no place to go, we wandered the streets. That's when I called the police, and they reached out to find a shelter for the night. That shelter became home, a place for help.

I didn't know that my father had begun discussions with Guy. He expressed concerns about my situation. Since I was not a citizen of Belgium, he feared being held responsible if anything happened to me or Amina. He told the authorities he had invited me to Belgium once to meet his family for three weeks. He was not responsible for my stay during my second visit, and Guy brought me to Brussels.

My father worried that his and Brigitte's financial stability, including their retirement, would be affected if I remained in Belgium. He didn't want to support me and my daughter. To protect himself, he urged Guy to start the process to have me deported back to Cameroon.

When Guy refused to comply with my father's instructions, he went to the justice system. He filed documentation stating he was not liable for me. He viewed our marriage as a white marriage and insisted on my deportation, wanting nothing to do with us.

My father asked my cousin Leto to cease all communication with me. He warned my siblings, Jaelle, Dorah, Corentin, and his wife, Brigitte, to avoid me entirely. Amina was perplexed by this rejection, creating a challenging situation for her. My father claimed I would never achieve anything, asserting that I had married Guy as a means of escape and labeling me a loser. He urged them to distance themselves from me, deepening our strain.

During this time, I traveled to Atlanta frequently per year with Amina. The visits with Elso built our connection. He encouraged me to apply for the DV lottery, and I decided to do it. As we discussed our future, I imagined what life could be like together.

One day, everything changed. On my way to work as a paralegal, I was arrested. Officials took my paperwork and placed me in transit, preparing to send me back to Cameroon. I contacted the judge I worked for, knowing she could help me.

She got me out the same and compiled the necessary paperwork to submit a request for citizenship, noting that my father was a Belgian citizen. However, that request was denied based on his filings.

The second option was to involve Guy. Although we were in the process of divorcing, our marriage wasn't finalized, and he was the only person who could counter my father's actions. The judge encouraged me to reach out to him.

I called Guy. He answered and rushed to help. When he arrived, he realized what was happening. Together, we went back to the mayor's office to fill out more forms, and they reinstated me with temporary paperwork until my permanent status was finalized.

At the same time, I received a brown envelope from United States Immigration notifying me that I had won the DV lottery. I opened it and read the instructions to return the paperwork within thirty days, listing the people I wanted to move to the United States with. The only person I had was Amina, so I filled it out and mailed it back.

However, I also received a call from Cameroon. My sister Rose informed me that my mother was ill and had HIV. This prompted me to get her a passport to bring her to Belgium.

After three months of waiting, my permanent card arrived. Excited and relieved, I went to pick up my mother at the airport. From there, I took her straight to the hospital for care. Within a few months, she recovered and gained weight. Amina, my mother, and I moved into my new home in Auderghem, leaving the shelter behind and starting our lives together.

As we settled in, I received a second letter with an appointment at the U.S. Embassy in Belgium stating that I had six months since I received my immigrant visa to leave the country.

The letter specified that I must meet all the requirements, pass a background check, demonstrate financial stability, and complete physical medical tests. I contacted Elso, who provided the necessary paperwork for the appointment. I booked our plane ticket, and once everything was set, Amina and I went to the embassy.

We spent the whole day there, arriving at nine a.m. and leaving at five p.m. We conducted several interviews, answered many questions, and successfully passed all the tests. We left the consulate with our immigrant visas stamped into our passports.

To qualify for a U.S. immigration visa, applicants must win the DV lottery, be twenty-one years old, hold a high school diploma, and pass a background check. Additionally, they must demonstrate financial stability, often by showing a minimum of twenty-five thousand dollars in a bank account for support during their initial months in the U.S. or have a sponsor willing to provide financial assistance.

These requirements may have changed, so for the most accurate information on the DV lottery and its current conditions, please visit the U.S. Immigration website.

With the fantastic news handy, I called my father again. "I'm going to the United States. I need you to help my mother while I'm gone." He did not support her, knowing she would need financial help and appointment assistance. Despite being the mother of his eldest child, he refused to take responsibility for Marthe.

He said he couldn't care for her. Instead, he offered to help me leave the country by selling my belongings. I agreed, knowing I had little choice. I didn't realize he was focused on his future. When he and Brigitte visited, they asked me to sign a power of attorney for her.

My father wanted the authority himself, which led to an argument. Brigitte claimed that being white would help sell my things faster.

Ultimately, I signed a power of attorney, allowing her to sell my home and car, pay my debts, and send me some money in the United States after covering their costs.

Helping me leave for the U.S. might give him a way in. As a musician, he had always dreamed of living in the U.S.; my opportunity was his chance. He rushed me to leave, not out of concern for me but to suit his plans.

Next, I focused on preparing for the move. I packed my life into boxes, organizing everything for the transition. I arranged a temporary place for my mother at a center where she could receive care and education until I stabilized my life in the United States and could bring her with me.

With everything moving forward. On February fourth, two thousand four, Amina and I went to the airport, checked our luggage, and got on the plane. We were leaving Brussels for Atlanta to start a new one.

Reflection

As I prepared to leave Belgium, I thought about the decisions that had led me here. My challenges shaped my path, and I learned to trust myself. Amina kept me grounded. Every step I took was for her future. The support from Elso helped me through my situation. As I moved to Atlanta, I held onto hope for a fresh start.

Conclusion

Humans are alone as a species in that we can experience hope, even in the worst situations. Through my formative years, subjected to abuse from so many people, hope was something I would never let go of. It was about taking back my life, step by step. With Amina beside me, every decision from this point would shape our future. The stakes were high, and I wanted stability to create a fear-free life. I was determined to build a life of joy, not just survival. I could almost see it in the quiet like light breaking through clouds. It was close, but the way forward wasn't simple.

Doubt stayed with me as I fastened my seatbelt on the flight to Atlanta, leaving Belgium behind as a place and a part of my life. The click of the seatbelt marked the choice to move forward. The plane's engines started, bringing my thoughts into focus. Everything I was leaving behind—every conversation, every decision, every mistake—stayed with me.

As the plane took off, I was between two worlds. Belgium faded below, but in my mind, it surged forward, pulling me back to moments that shaped me and who I could become. This was more than just moving from one place to another. The noise of the aircraft made my memories clear. I drifted into the past, each moment pulling at me, reminding me of what I was carrying. The recycled air couldn't shake those memories, now following me across oceans. I wasn't just leaving; I was moving toward something, though exactly what I hadn't yet figured out.

As the plane moved, the changes ahead needed direction. This was more than just a new location—it was a chance to reshape my life. Leaving what was behind became easier as I moved forward. My choices now would shape a life reflecting who I am. The plane's steady rise seemed tied to a shift within. The sounds and sensations pushed things forward. Each motion under the seatbelt was a reminder that life kept changing. There had been moments when life led down unexpected paths. But now, the way forward was one I chose, stepping into something that was mine. The clouds below drifted by, marking the movement of time. Each one seemed to carry a piece of the past with it. Belgium was now behind me, no longer holding me back. The memories of that time remained, not as burdens but as markers of what I had overcome.

I turned to look at Amina, her eyes closed, resting peacefully. She had been with me through so much. She knew the struggles I had faced, the losses and the quiet victories. When she noticed me looking, her smile said everything. It was her way of reminding me that I wasn't alone, no matter what came next.

The thought of what waited in Atlanta brought both excitement and uncertainty. Instead of feeling overwhelmed, I was driven by what lay ahead. Every moment felt like progress. This wasn't just moving forward but reclaiming what had been lost. As the space between where I was and where I could be grown, it felt like moving further from what was behind. Something new was ahead. I knew there would be obstacles, but I would handle them my way this time. The path was open, waiting to be shaped. After a long time, I was ready to take action.

To understand my journey, it's important to look back at the early experiences that shaped my life. The threat of abandonment runs deep, stretching through generations of my family before I even had words for it. My grandfather's absence left a mark on our family, forcing my grandmother to raise her children alone while he fathered more children elsewhere. The impact of that abandonment became an inheritance, passed down without explanation.

For me, abandonment came early. My father disappeared when I was born, leaving only questions behind. My mother, just 14 at the time, struggled with motherhood. By the time I was two, she had also left, starting a different life far from me. She had two more children, Rose and Babou, with her boyfriend, Daniel. I often wondered what life was like for them, a family I wasn't part of. While I stayed behind, my grandmother stepped in, taking on the responsibility my parents couldn't handle.

The memories of those early years are faint but leave a lasting mark. I remember watching doors close—my mother's and my father's—leaving a silence that felt louder than words. It was my grandmother's hands and her presence that kept me connected to something steady. Even as a child, the feeling of being left behind sank in, shaping how I saw the world and my place in it.

From when I was two until I was ten, I lived with my Uncle Baboulek in his large home. It gave me stability after a chaotic past. The ceilings were high, and light streamed through the windows. The change from feeling abandoned to finding security with my uncle was something I understood much later.

My uncle was strict, but his care showed in how he structured our lives and the lessons he gave. Each task had a purpose, and I learned through his actions. Every day had its rhythm, and knowing what to expect brought peace. My grandmother was also a guiding figure. In the evenings, she would tell me stories passed down through our family, offering lessons about family and perseverance. Those stories became the foundation I relied on during my life's toughest times.

I lived with my uncle for eight years, where hard work and wisdom were central to my upbringing. But the stability I had known disappeared when I was sent to live with my Aunt Régine. What could have been a continuation of care turned into mistreatment and pain. The streets of Yaoundé became my escape, offering some freedom despite the risks.

At 11, my life changed again when Bernard found me on the streets. Those streets had made me grow up quickly and taught me how to survive. When Bernard offered me a home, it gave me hope. Since my time with my uncle, I hadn't known what it felt like to have a stable home. But just as things began to settle, life shifted again.

My mother, remarried and living in Yokaduma, sent my half-siblings, Rose and Babou, to live with me. I was still a child, learning to stand on my own. Suddenly, I was expected to take care of them. My mother had moved on, and it felt like she handed me the responsibility of raising her children. I was still working through my struggles, now faced with protecting Rose and Babou from the same hardships I had barely escaped.

Caring for them wasn't just a task but a test of my ability to give love even though I had received so little. I wanted them to feel something I had rarely experienced: knowing someone was there for them. The responsibility was a lot to carry, especially for a child still figuring out her path, but I took it on because I had to. Every moment brought its own set of difficulties, but small moments, like when Rose smiled or when Babou looked at me, reminded me that even though I didn't have all the answers, I was doing the right thing.

As a teenager, I wrestled with my mother's life choices, torn between wanting to understand her and not wanting to follow in her footsteps. Each visit to Yoka Duma, where she lived with Henry, felt like entering a different world—one where love was marked by control and abuse. The tension in their home was always there, like a storm about to break. I would watch my mother move through the house, her eyes telling the story of a life she didn't choose.

The bruises she tried to hide, the silence after Henry's words, said it all. Every moment in that house, she made me more determined. I couldn't let myself end up trapped like she had. I refused to be part of that chain of suffering.

During this time, I discovered something that changed everything. I found out about my biological father, Bachot, living in Belgium. It felt like uncovering a part of myself that had been missing. Thoughts of him stirred feelings of anger, curiosity, and hope. What would he be like? Would meeting him give me the answers I was looking for? The discovery was like opening a door to a past I had never known.

At 15, my life shifted again. I started a relationship with Elso, and soon after, we had our daughter, Amina. Becoming a mother at such a young age was overwhelming. Holding Amina for the first time made everything worth it. She became a reason to keep going. Motherhood, though challenging, gave me purpose. Between caring for Amina and trying to figure out my own life, there were days I felt lost. But somehow, I kept going.

Around that time, I traveled to Brussels to meet my biological father, Bachot. It felt like I was uncovering a part I had never known. Meeting him stirred many emotions—anger, curiosity, and hope. Who was this man? Would meeting him answer questions about who I was? I stayed with him for three weeks, trying to piece together my past and present.

Brussels, though impressive, didn't feel like home. It was like I was visiting a life that wasn't mine. When I returned to Cameroon, I had more questions than answers. People expected me to return with success, but I had none of that. Their expectations left me feeling out of place, disconnected from everything I had known.

Not long after I returned, Elso left for the United States without a word. His disappearance shook me. One day, he was there, and the next, he was gone, leaving me to raise our daughter alone. We stayed in touch for six months, but then the calls stopped. I was left wondering if he was gone for good. Every day felt like a struggle to keep going and find a way forward without him.

During this time, I often went to a cyber cafe, where I met Guy online. Our conversations started simple but grew into something deeper. He supported me in ways I hadn't expected.

Eventually, I joined him in Belgium, leaving behind my life in Cameroon. We got married, and for a time, I felt secure. But soon, the past resurfaced. On my wedding day, Elso called. Hearing his voice brought back everything I thought I had left behind. Soon after, I found his messages, each stirring emotion I thought I had moved past. His words made it impossible to close the door to that part of my life.

At 18, I entered what I thought was adulthood, marrying Guy, who was 43. The age difference was clear, but I convinced myself it didn't matter, that love or circumstances would bridge the gap. As time passed, it became clear that I was still young, still figuring out who I was, while Guy had lived through years of experiences I couldn't fully understand. I tried to play the role of an adult, but deep down, I knew I was still learning how to handle life, love, and responsibilities.

At the same time, I was traveling to the United States regularly to visit Amina's father, Elso. These trips reminded me of something I had lost—a part of myself I hadn't seen in years. On my third visit, things between Elso and me changed. What had once faded into the past became real again. We rekindled something I thought was long gone, and for the first time in years, I felt alive and connected. It was messy and complicated, but it reminded me I could feel something beyond the numbness I had grown used to in my marriage. When Guy sensed that I was pulling away, his desperation grew. He wasn't ready to let go, and his attempts to hold on to what was left of our marriage became more forceful. He pleaded with me, offering to let me stay in the house, suggesting I could move upstairs, and we could live separately under the same roof. But I knew his offer wasn't about making things work—it was about control. He didn't want to lose his hold over me, and I wasn't willing to stay in a situation where I had no real space to be myself. The idea of staying in the same house, stuck in a relationship that was suffocating me, was unbearable.

The tension between us was always there, even though we slept in separate rooms. I could sense him nearby, watching, waiting for a chance to confront me. It wasn't peaceful; it was a reminder of the conflict behind every interaction. Every night, I lay awake, listening for his footsteps, wondering when the next argument would come.

I threw myself into school, managing the house, and trying to create a routine, but even that seemed empty. After dinner, I would sit with Amina, just the two of us, while he and his son lived separately in the same house. We existed in a broken world where nothing seemed real or safe. I avoided being around Guy as much as possible. I spent most of my time in my room, trying to find peace, but I couldn't escape him even then.

He would follow me, listening to my phone calls, waiting for me to slip up. One day, during a call with Elso, I said, "I love you," not realizing Guy was outside the door listening. His reaction was instant and violent. He stormed out of the house, his anger clear. I followed, needing to get away and breathe, but it didn't matter how far I ran—his anger followed me like a stab.

When I tried to return to the house, Guy grabbed me. His hands were rough, his grip tight. It wasn't just the physical act that scared me but the look in his eyes. At that moment, I saw he wasn't just angry—he was desperate and out of control. I knew I wasn't safe here. I wasn't free with him. I was living where fear ruled, and there was no room for me.

I felt panic rise inside me, but I couldn't move, couldn't breathe. My mind raced with questions. What would happen if I stayed? What would happen to Amina if I didn't leave?

At that point, everything was clear. I had to leave for Amina and myself. Staying meant losing who I was. I pulled away from Guy, knowing I had to make my escape. It wasn't just about leaving the house but about taking back my life. I didn't know what was ahead, but I couldn't live in fear anymore. I called my father, telling him I was going to his place in La Basilique.

My voice shook as I tried to stay calm, hoping he would understand. But when I arrived, his refusal was immediate. His face was cold, and I felt another door close, leaving me outside with my daughter and nowhere to turn. The rejection hit me hard. I had thought, despite everything, that my father would be there when I needed him most.

We left his house and went down the stairwell, our footsteps filling the space. Outside, the night stretched ahead, vast and unwelcoming. The streetlights barely cut through the darkness, and each corner reminded me how alone I was. I had no plans, no safety net. My daughter held my hand, and I clung to a small hope that something would change.

In desperation, I called the police. It felt like admitting I couldn't fight this alone. When they arrived, they didn't need every detail. They just helped. Their kindness gave me the support I hadn't expected. They took us to La Maison des Femmes Battues, a shelter for women like me. It wasn't home, but it was safe, and that was more than I had felt in a long time.

At the shelter, life followed a pattern. My daughter and I shared a small room. It wasn't much—just a queen bed, a table, and a chair—but it was a space where I could close the door, and, for a moment, we were okay. The walls were thin, and sometimes, the sounds of women talking or crying carried through the hall, but inside our room, there was peace. Meals were served at specific times: breakfast at 7, lunch at noon, and dinner at 7. If you missed one, you had to wait. The strict schedule gave me something steady.

I looked forward to those meals, not for the food, but because they provided structure. Even with the limitations, I didn't let the shelter define our future. After my daughter fell asleep each night, I sat at the table and studied law. The small room was filled with my books, and though the dim light strained my eyes, I kept going. I had to build a life for us, one where we wouldn't depend on anyone. Studying law was my way forward, a way to protect us from ever being in this situation again.

My paralegal job helped me save money. Every penny had to stretch as I balanced studying, working, and caring for Amina. It was tiring, but it had to be done. Each small step moved me closer to a better life. To make ends meet, I took a second job as a receptionist at La Forêt de Soignes (Sonian Forest), a high-end gym. Walking through its sleek doors daily was like stepping into a different world. The polished floors, the lights, the smell of fresh towels—a world far removed from the shelter. The clients came to unwind while I worked to hold everything together. It was like living two separate lives—one full of work, the other of ease—but the paycheck made it worth it.

Even with the exhausting hours, I found moments of reflection during my shift at Alpharetta Swine. I saw how much I could endure. The long hours, the two jobs, and the sleepless nights laid a foundation for something greater—small sacrifices for a future I could almost grasp. Though shelter life was challenging, it offered me a space to rebuild.

The predictability helped me think more clearly. I worked steadily, and with each shift and law book, I started to reclaim parts of myself. Surviving shifted to making plans. Watching my daughter sleep in that small room, I knew I had to keep going.

There was still a long way to go, but I felt like I was moving in the right direction, creating independence for both of us. I didn't know that my father, Bachot, was already working behind the scenes—setting events in motion that would undo all I had worked for.

Bachot had been having discussions about me. These weren't about supporting me through one of the most challenging times of my life. Instead, his focus was on self-preservation. He wasn't concerned about Amina or me but about how my stay might affect him. He feared that he would be held responsible if anything happened to us. His concerns weren't about our safety but the disruption we posed. He shared his version of events with the authorities, painting a story that suited his needs. He said I had been invited to Belgium for a short visit to meet his family, which should have been the end. But, as he put it, I came back.

It became obvious that he never intended for me to stay. I was a guest, not family. Over time, I shifted from being his daughter to becoming a burden. He worried I would disrupt the life he and Brigitte had built. Together, they discussed ways to remove me from their world.

Deportation seemed like the answer. My father wasn't content with cutting ties emotionally—he wanted me gone. The possibility of me staying wasn't something he could face. To him, it was easier to push me away than to accept the reality of having me close. I wasn't seen as a daughter who needed help but a problem to be solved.

While trying to create a future for us, I saw that my father wasn't simply absent—he was working against me. He refused to help and instead tried to erase me from his life. The realization that I wasn't just unwanted emotionally but also physically was something I could never have prepared for. His betrayal changed my view of family, forcing me to confront the harsh truth that those you expect to rely on can become the ones who hurt you most. It was a painful lesson, but I had no choice but to accept it.

My father made his decision, and I had to make mine. Holding onto the hope that he would see me as his daughter again was no longer an option. I had to move on, focusing on the future, even if that meant doing it alone. As more challenges came, I knew fighting for a better future would be harder than I imagined. When Guy refused to comply with the divorce, my father's actions deepened the rift. Instead of offering support, he filed documents to distance himself from me. It felt like he was erasing me from his life, officially and permanently.

In those documents, my marriage to Guy was reduced to a strategic arrangement I had supposedly created to stay in Belgium. His words stayed with me; each one aimed at my character. He claimed I had no genuine connection to Guy, that I had only married him for convenience, to secure a place where I didn't belong. According to him, my entire life was a fraud, a scam. Worse, he told the court I was worthless and would never amount to anything. Hearing this from my father—a man who should have been my protector—felt like the deepest betrayal. It wasn't just about the lies he told about me or my marriage; it was how he broke me down, stripping away any dignity I had left. I found myself fighting the system or Guy and my own family—the people who should have stood by me in my darkest moments.

But my father didn't stop at filing the papers. He took additional steps to isolate me entirely. He told my cousin Leto to cut all communication with me. It felt like he was dismantling my support, piece by piece. He didn't stop there, though. He also warned my siblings, Jaelle, Dorah, and Corentin, to stay away from me. He was making sure I would be in this fight alone.

Then there was Brigitte, my father's wife. She made it clear I no longer belonged with them. She erased any connection to their world. The separation ran deep. Any hope of reconciliation faded. My father ensured no one in the family would support me. I went from being a daughter, a cousin, and a sister to becoming a memory. There were no phone calls, no messages. I had been cut off completely.

I faced a painful truth: the people I once relied on were now cutting ties. My father's actions weren't only about legal matters. He made sure I would be removed from their lives. He didn't want me in Belgium or his circle. And he ensured the rest of the family followed him. This went beyond abandonment—it was an effort to erase me. The betrayal was real, but I couldn't let it shape my identity. I had to move forward for Amina and myself.

As I moved forward, their actions weighed heavily on us. Amina struggled as her world changed, and what they did affected both of us. While I tried to protect her from the pain of being pushed aside, I could feel it changing how I saw people and the world. Their actions broke what family and love were supposed to be. For Amina, the confusion caused by being ignored by those who should have cared was clear. I saw it in her eyes as she looked at me, silently asking why they turned away and pretended we weren't there. It wasn't just confusion—it was something more profound, and I felt it, too.

Their actions made me question everything I thought I knew. If those meant to love and protect us could turn away so quickly, what did that mean for others? It went beyond family, forcing me to reconsider everything about trust, loyalty, and human connections. The world seemed colder. The connections I once relied on now felt fragile, as if they could break at any moment, much like how my family had turned away from us.

This experience left marks on both of us. For Amina, it was a painful lesson about family and love, one I had tried hard to protect her from. For me, it was a harsh reminder that those you expect to stand by can be the ones to hurt you most. That knowledge stays with you, altering how you see the world and people. The pain didn't only come from being pushed away. It came from realizing that nothing could be taken for granted—not even love.

While everything with my father and family ties unraveled, I found hope elsewhere. My trips to the United States, where Amina spent time with her father, Elso, gave me a break from the weight I carried. It felt like returning to a time when things were simpler when warmth and connection were still present. On each visit, I saw Amina grow in Elso's presence. Their bond felt natural, showing me that not all relationships were broken. His love for Amina remained true, untouched by the complexities of the past. It showed me that family could still exist without bitterness.

These visits brought something back within me I hadn't expected. Being with Elso brought memories of our childhood in Cameroon. Each shared moment pulled me back to a time before things became difficult—before my father's choices and the loneliness of recent years. We would walk, talk about the past, and laugh at things that once seemed trivial. Gradually, something between us changed. The focus shifted from Amina to us—what we had shared and what we might still create.

Then came the moment that changed everything. It seemed like an ordinary day as we walked through Olympic Park. Amina ran ahead, laughing. The sun was setting, and for a brief moment, everything felt right, like I was exactly where I needed to be. But then Elso stopped. He reached into his pocket and pulled out a small velvet box. My heart raced. I wasn't prepared for this. I was still married to Guy, and my mind was spinning. Elso knelt down and opened the box to reveal a diamond ring.

The world around me seemed to blur; all I could focus on was him. His eyes held so much hope and love. I never thought I would see that again, not after everything I had been through. But here he was, asking me to marry him. I knew I was still married to Guy, but I didn't know how to say no to the crowd around us. I didn't want to embarrass him, so I said yes, even though I knew it wasn't simple.

The tears in my eyes weren't just about the moment. They were about to realize that love could still find me. The crowd cheered, and strangers shared in the moment, but I knew I would have to face the reality of my situation soon.

During our time together, Elso and I explored the city, shared meals, and discussed our future. He often brought up our conversations from Cameroon, where we imagined a life free from the religious pressure that had always been around us. In Cameroon, as Muslims and Christians, our relationship went against what was expected. From the start, we knew we were stepping outside the norms of what our families and society accepted.

There were many moments of tension where we had to explain ourselves not just to others but to each other. We weren't fighting only for love; we were fighting for our right to exist together in a world that didn't see us as a match. Elso's proposal became a promise of freedom, offering the chance to live the life we had always dreamed of, even with the challenges of my situation with Guy.

The family held onto their expectations, and we were often reminded that we were meant to stay within the boundaries of our respective faiths. Tradition said I, as a Christian, should marry a Christian man, and Elso, as a Muslim, was expected to find a wife within his faith. To do otherwise was seen as disrespectful to our upbringing and the generations before us. Whispers followed us, disapproval from elders, and confusion from those who couldn't understand why we would take such a risk.

People didn't just question our faith; they questioned everything, including my situation with Guy. When I accepted Elso's proposal, my family and others disapproved of me still being married, adding more judgment to an already tense situation. In that moment, I had to balance my inner conflict and the external expectations that had shaped our relationship. We always knew we were challenging what our families and society considered suitable, and their disapproval weighed on every decision.

Elso's proposal, despite its timing and complications, represented the freedom we longed for—a life where we set our own rules, free from the constraints that had always tried to define us.

The family held onto their expectations, and we were often reminded that we were meant to stay within the boundaries of our respective faiths. Tradition said I, as a Christian, should marry a Christian man, and Elso, as a Muslim, was expected to find a wife within his faith. To do otherwise was seen as disrespectful to our upbringing and the generations before us. Whispers followed us, disapproval from elders, and confusion from those who couldn't understand why we would take such a risk.

People didn't just question our faith; they questioned everything, including my situation with Guy. When I accepted Elso's proposal, my family and others disapproved of me still being married, adding more judgment to an already tense situation. In that moment, I had to balance my inner conflict and the external expectations that had shaped our relationship. We always knew we were challenging what our families and society considered right, and their disapproval weighed on every decision.

Elso's proposal, despite its timing and complications, represented the freedom we longed for—a life where we set our own rules, free from the constraints that had always tried to define us.

Blending our cultures meant creating something entirely our own. We imagined a home rich with both our backgrounds, where the aroma of our favorite Cameroonian dishes reminded us of where we came from. Prayers would be spoken in Arabic,

French, English, and our dialects. Amina would hear stories from both faiths, embracing every part of her identity while honoring where we came from and moving forward.

America, with all its imperfections, became a place where we could build a life without feeling like we were on the outside. Here, we could create our path without constantly looking back or worrying about what others thought. I believe we had left behind cultural and familial expectations for a time. But even as we embraced this freedom, the unresolved situation with Guy remained in the background, a reminder that some ties to my past in Belgium still held me back.

We could be free, and with that freedom, we found hope—hope that Amina could live the life she deserved, where she could embrace both her Muslim and Christian roots and her African and American identities without feeling divided. Even as we held onto that dream, I was aware of Guy's situation. It weighed on me, but the vision of a better life for Amina kept us moving forward, focused on creating a life free from the constraints that had shaped us.

As we walked and talked about our future, I realized Elso's question was about more than marriage. It meant building the life we had always envisioned. For the first time, it wasn't just a dream—it felt within reach. We had made it through difficult times, and now, we were ready to create something lasting that was indeed ours. But life didn't slow down.

When I returned to Belgium, and the shelter where Amina and I had been staying, the difference between the hope I felt with Elso and the reality of our situation became clearer. The joy of what we shared was still fresh in my mind, but returning to the shelter reminded me of the unfinished parts of my life, especially my marriage with Guy. I felt pulled between two worlds—one full of hope, the other still tied to parts of my past.

Living in the shelter had been necessary for survival, but it was merely existing, not truly living. I had been waiting for something better, for the next step. I wanted something real, not just temporary solutions. Elso sparked in me a longing for something permanent. Our bond had grown strong through everything we had faced. But love alone couldn't provide the foundation I needed. I craved a place where we wouldn't have to worry about where we would be next month or year. Drifting wasn't an option anymore—I needed a place to settle. Dealing with Guy's ongoing situation and divorce added to the urgency. The shelter had played its part, but I needed a place of my own, somewhere to build a future. Owning a home meant more than just a space to live in—it was the first step toward something secure, something I could rely on.

Sitting in that shelter, I knew it was time to act. My savings had reached a point where buying a home felt within reach, a concrete goal. I felt like I had options and the power to change our situation. It wasn't just about leaving the shelter; it was about making choices that would secure a future for Amina and me, something lasting. I couldn't let this chance slip away. I needed to turn that sense of empowerment into a reality to create a foundation to provide us with what we needed.

As I walked out of the bank that day, I felt something new hope through action. No more dreaming. It was about making it real. The shelter had been a place of waiting, but now I had a clear direction. I could see a future not shaped by the past but by where I was headed. Back at the shelter, in the quiet moments when Amina slept, I'd sit by the window and imagine the home

I would buy. I could picture it—Amina with her room, us sharing meals in our kitchen. Where Elso could visit, and we'd plan for the future without fear. It was more than a house. It marked the start of a chapter shaped by my choices for our future.

It was for us. It was for the life I wanted my daughter to have. I wanted her to grow up feeling safe and permanent. I wanted her to have security, which I never knew. I wanted her to understand that she had a place to call home no matter what. This was about more than the present; it was the future we could build together. A home wasn't simply a building but the foundation of everything I had worked toward.

But then, everything changed. One day, while driving to work, officials stopped me for what seemed like a routine check. At first, I wasn't concerned, but I saw an issue as they went through my documents. My residency papers had expired, and suddenly, the reality of the situation became clear.

When I married Guy, I was supposed to visit the mayor's office within 90 days to extend my residency as his spouse. But instead of staying in our home, I left and moved into the shelter. Living there, struggling to survive, I lost track of what I needed to do to keep my legal status. The chance to update my papers had slipped away due to our separation, leaving me without legal standing. Suddenly, my progress and the future I was building felt shaky. The home I was close to securing, the stability I wanted for Amina, now seemed like it could unravel. I hadn't expected how quickly everything could change. After all the work I had put in, it now felt like I was on the edge of losing it all.

I felt frustrated—at the situation, myself, and everything that had forced me into this position. I had worked hard to get here, and another hurdle was being placed in my way. But beyond frustration, there was fear. Could I stay? What would happen to the future I had envisioned for Amina? This could change everything. I needed to act fast to fix this, but there were no guarantees. The stakes were high, not just for me but for Amina and the life I wanted for her.

The situation tested everything I had been working toward. Legal paperwork was only part of it; the bigger picture was the life I had been building from the ground up. Even with the fear, I wasn't ready to give up. I had fought for Amina's future and couldn't let her down now. The situation had serious consequences. My father had filed paperwork to have me deported, putting me on the radar of the authorities. When the officers found my expired documents, everything escalated quickly. I was detained and placed in transit, with preparations underway to send me back. At that moment, everything seemed to be slipping away. But I refused to let the panic take over. I had to act.

Since I had left the marital home and moved into the shelter, I had focused on survival rather than the administrative tasks that now hung over my future. I laid out my situation for her, hoping she could offer some guidance or a way to help me extend my time. Deep down, I understood how crucial this moment had become.

I laid it all out for her, hoping she could offer guidance or a solution to buy me more time. I knew this was a critical moment. I was fighting for Amina. Every second in detention made the future I had been working toward more distant. My dreams of creating a home and building a life were hanging by a thread. I didn't realize then that my father had already complicated things behind the scenes by filing paperwork. That truth wouldn't come to light until later. At that moment, all I knew was that I needed someone on my side to help me navigate a system working against me.

The judge listened carefully. I could tell from her measured tone that she was already thinking about my steps. She didn't promise an immediate resolution—there were no guarantees—but she vowed to do what she could. Her calm voice gave me hope when I needed it most.

As I hung up, I knew the battle wasn't over. Time was running out, and while I had reached out for help, there was no certainty about what would come next. I was caught between immigration laws and the life I had built, and the gap felt impossible to bridge. But I held on to the small glimmer of hope that my call had brought—a lifeline in the chaos. Another wave hit before I could process the relief from speaking to the judge. My phone rang again. This time, it was Baroon. My mother's voice was urgent, filled with distress.

My mother was calling about her sister, Régine. Régine had embezzled a significant amount of money from her job and needed 2 million CFA, about 3,200 U.S. dollars, to fix the situation. My mother pleaded, saying only I could help. The amount felt impossible, but the emotional weight of her request was even more pressing.

She wasn't just asking for financial help; she was asking me to set aside the years of mistreatment Régine had put me through. My mother's words brought back memories I had tried to forget. Régine had told me I was nothing and would never amount to anything. Those words had driven me, pushing me to prove her wrong. Now, she was the one in trouble, and my mother was asking me to be the one to offer help.

But deep down, I knew holding on to that pain wouldn't serve me. I had come too far to let bitterness anchor me to the past. After careful thought, I chose a path I hadn't expected. I forgave Régine. It wasn't easy, but it felt necessary—not for her, but for me. Letting go of that weight freed me from the shadows of her past actions. Once I decided, I sent my mother the money to help Régine out of her situation.

It was a strange moment, knowing I had done what was asked of me but also realizing this wasn't just about the money. It was about moving forward. Forgiveness didn't mean forgetting, but it meant reclaiming my power and right to move on without being tied to the pain of the past.

While I was navigating the decision with Régine, other parts of my life were still hanging in the balance. Fortunately, the judge temporarily got me out of the transit, halting the process of sending me back. She submitted the necessary paperwork to the immigration office, hoping to use my father's Belgian citizenship to resolve the situation, but the request was denied. Only later did I find out why—my father had already filed against me.

The judge told me my best chance was to involve Guy, who I was still legally married to. Despite our separation and the painful history between us, our divorce wasn't finalized, and he was the only one who could lawfully intervene and counter what my father had done.

The realization hit hard. Here I was, building a future with Elso, dreaming of a life where love and stability could finally coexist, but still tied to Guy by the complications of the past. I needed Guy's legal help, but it felt strange and conflicting, knowing that while my heart was with Elso, I had to rely on Guy to protect my future. It was another reminder of how intertwined the past and present had become and how difficult it was to break free and move forward fully.

Elso had given me hope for a new chapter, but Guy still had legal power over my immediate future. The tension lingered, balancing what had been and what could be.

I hesitated before making the call but knew it had to be done. When Guy picked up, I laid everything out. "Guy, I need your help," I said, the words spilling out quickly. There was a pause on the other end before he responded.

"I already know what's happening. Your father contacted me. He wants me to agree to have you deported, but I refused."

I was stunned. Why would my father do that?

"He thinks it's best for everyone, but I don't. I think you're better off staying in Belgium, and I'll do whatever I can to ensure that happens. Whether we're together as husband and wife, I don't want you to leave."

His words hit me harder than I expected. The man who had caused me so much pain was now standing up for me, offering something I hadn't anticipated—support.

"I'm sorry, Cara," he continued, his voice softer than I'd heard in a long time. "For everything. The things I did, the way

I hurt you… I'll never be able to take that back, but I will do right by you this time. You don't deserve this. I'll help you."

His voice was sincere, a tone I hadn't heard in so long. Guy had always been brutal, always unpredictable, but now, in this moment, he seemed genuine. I couldn't help but think of Elso. The contrast between them was stark—Elso offered me love and hope for a future, while Guy offered me a lifeline in a crisis. Could I have ever expected Guy to be the one standing beside me now, especially after all he had done?

He promised to meet me at the office with the judge to help resolve the situation. Together, as instructed by the judge, we went to the mayor's office and completed the necessary forms to stabilize my case. It wasn't easy, but having him there allowed me to move forward. I thought it strange that I was leaning on Guy to help me stay in Belgium while trying to build a future with Elso. My heart felt torn between two worlds—one rooted in the past and the other in the promise of something new.

When I left the office that day, I walked out with temporary paperwork, allowing me to stay in Belgium until my permanent status could be processed. Leaving the mayor's office with that paperwork in hand gave me a moment to breathe. I had more time to stay, figure things out, and continue building the life I had been fighting for. But now, I also knew this was only a temporary solution, and the uncertainty about my future in Belgium was far from over. There were still challenges ahead, and this was just the beginning.

As I stepped into the street, I glanced at Guy. We had just come through one of the most challenging moments of my life, and somehow, he had been part of the solution. It felt strange—the same person who had caused me so much pain had now helped me stay, at least for a bit longer. I felt both thankful and cautious. We weren't together, and this didn't change our history. Elso was still the person I wanted a future with, but Guy's support mattered at this moment. It reminded me that life is rarely straightforward, and sometimes, the people you least expect show up when you need them most.

Guy gave me a nod, acknowledging what had happened between us without needing to say anything more. He had played his part, and now we were both ready to go our separate ways. I looked down at the documents in my hand. They were temporary but represented an opportunity for Amina and me to keep moving forward. Every decision I made from here out would be about securing our futures. The next few days were filled with gathering documents, preparing for interviews, and completing the legal steps I needed to finalize my status. Each task brought me closer to the goal, step by step.

I had come a long way from living in a shelter and facing deportation to standing here with a chance to move forward. The paperwork might have been temporary, but it gave me something to hold on to. It wasn't everything, but it was enough to keep me going. I had hoped that soon Amina and I would achieve the stability we had fought so hard for, but just when I thought I had found a direction, life brought something unexpected.

I received a brown envelope from U.S. Immigration. I saw that the document inside could change everything as I opened it. I had secured the diversity lottery program. The lottery, offering visas to individuals from countries with low immigration rates, was a rare opportunity to start over in the United States. The instructions were clear. I had 30 days to complete and return the paperwork listing the people I wanted to bring with me. It was an easy decision. The only person I wanted with me was Amina.

Even as I filled out the lottery paperwork, the thought of Elso stayed with me. We had started planning a future together, but Guy's help keeping me in Belgium added a new dimension. I was grateful to Guy for standing by me when I needed him, but my heart was with Elso. Balancing these relationships while trying to plan a future for Amina and me felt like a delicate process. The lottery brought opportunity but also added responsibility. I was handling temporary residency in Belgium, planning our future, and now considering relocating to the U.S.

I knew that every decision I made from this point on had to be thoughtful. The diversity lottery gave me a chance but also meant I had to be prepared for the next steps. The path to securing a future for Amina and myself felt more important than ever.

As I sent off the papers for the immigration lottery, I thought about what this move could mean for us: a real chance to give Amina the life she deserved. But it wouldn't be easy. Winning the lottery was just a step forward, with more challenges ahead. Staying focused and ready for whatever came next was crucial. The possibility of a new future felt real, but nothing was certain. I had to keep moving forward to secure a better life for Amina. Just as I was planning for this, a call came from Cameroon. It was my sister Rose, and her voice carried worry. She told me our mother had been very sick, something she hadn't been able to say to me until now. My heart sank as I asked how long this had been going on, but Rose couldn't answer me.

The uncertainty gnawed at me, knowing the distance made it even harder to help. I sent money right away for my mom to have medical tests done. Days later, when they called again, the news wasn't good. My mom had been diagnosed with HIV. This added to everything I was already handling but supporting her became a priority. Even as I focused on building a future for us, I felt the need to be there for her to ensure she was taken care of.

I sent more money to help her get a passport, hoping she could come to Belgium for better treatment. I wanted her to have the best care possible. Around the same time, I visited homes in Anderlecht and other areas, searching for a place that would work for us. After seeing several options, I found the right one—a two-bedroom, two-bathroom house with a yard in Auderghem. It wasn't just a home but a chance to start fresh.

After three months, my permanent residency card arrived, and I received the finalized divorce papers. The card symbolized everything I had fought for, and knowing our future in Belgium was secure brought relief. As I finalized the house purchase, I began planning the space for us, choosing colors and furniture to make it our own. While there was joy in building this new home, I was also preparing for the reality of my mom's condition.

In Cameroon, HIV carries a heavy stigma. People living with the virus were often shunned and left on their own because the community didn't understand it. If my mother's diagnosis became known, she would face judgment and abandonment. I couldn't let that happen. That's why I acted quickly to bring her to Belgium, to shield her from the prejudice she would face at home. I wanted her to be safe, far from the rejection and shame surrounding her.

I prepared a room for her, ensuring the kitchen had her favorite foods from a shop in Matongue, Brussels. I wanted her to feel at home immediately, to recognize the smells, tastes, and teas she loved. Every detail mattered. I hoped being close to me would give her peace, knowing she was cared for. As the day approached, I felt both eager and anxious. I wanted to care for her in person finally, but I also knew her health was fragile. I allowed myself to hope that coming to Belgium might make a difference.

On the day of her flight, I went to the airport, ready to greet her. I imagined her journey, wondering what thoughts filled her mind as she headed to Belgium—the hours stretched as I waited by the gate. When her flight landed, I watched the crowd, my heart racing. And then, I saw her. She looked tired from the trip but seeing her in person made everything else fade away. I hugged her, holding her close, knowing this was the start of something new. The road ahead wouldn't be easy, but at that moment, it was just about being together.

Even with fear, my mother faced everything with strength. She didn't let the illness define her, and I respected that. She still found joy and carried herself with dignity. Seeing her confidence return helped me push through the worry. It reminded me why we were doing all of this—for her to live and for us to live with her. Her resilience gave me the strength to keep going, even when it was hard.

As the captain's voice came through the speakers, signaling we were nearing our destination, I opened my eyes slowly, adjusting to the present moment. Amina was next to me, sleeping soundly. I watched her, thankful for her presence and the new chapter ahead. This move was as much for her as it was for me: a chance to give her the future we had dreamed of. My thoughts went back to my mother. Though she wasn't on this flight, her recovery and strength reassured me. Leaving her behind had been hard, but it was time for Amina and me to move forward.

I looked out the window as we got closer. The journey was almost over, and the life we worked for was within reach. Atlanta was no longer just a hope—it was real, and we were nearly there. The captain spoke again, and I felt quiet excitement, knowing we'd soon arrive. There would be challenges, but we were ready.

She shared stories about her life in Cameroon and the realities of being in polygamous marriages, which had shaped many of her choices. Each moment we spent together became meaningful, as I started to see her not just as a figure from my childhood but as a woman with her own experiences. Leaving for the United States was difficult. I worried that our newfound bond would be lost. Her health had improved, and I was beginning to connect with her truly.

As I prepared for my move, I felt torn. I wanted to be part of her life in Belgium; to support her in ways I hadn't been able to, but I also knew I needed to focus on my future in America. It was a difficult balance to strike, but I had to decide to respect our lives.

I reached out to my father, hoping he could support her while I was away. We met at a café near La Basilique, where I explained the situation—her illness, her improvement since moving to Belgium, and my plans to leave for the U.S. I asked if he could help her during my transition. His response wasn't what I expected. After years of distance, he seemed willing to consider it, though he gave no firm commitment. He asked questions about her condition and treatment, and while the conversation felt somewhat detached, I was relieved that he accepted the idea outright.

As I left the café, I reflected on the years of silence between us. I didn't expect this moment to fix everything, but it felt like a step. There was still so much to figure out before my move, but knowing he might offer some support gave me a bit of reassurance as I continued walking through the streets of La Basilique.

With the plane to Atlanta still in progress, I looked at Amina resting beside me, thinking about what this move would mean for us. It was a step towards something new and a leap into the unknown. There were no guarantees; I only hoped things would work out for us in the United States and my mother in Belgium.

After speaking with my father, I knew I needed to find another way to ensure my mother was cared for while I was away. That's when I contacted the social workers at La Maison des Femmes Battues. I explained my concerns about her health and my upcoming move. One of the social workers offered a solution I hadn't thought of—she told me about a center where my mother would receive the care she needed, from attending doctor's appointments to getting her prescriptions. They would even help her with the transition to join me in the U.S. when the time came.

It was the solution I had been looking for. Visiting the center in person, I found it clean, well-organized, and precisely what I had hoped. I left knowing my mother would be well-looked.

After leaving the center and arranging everything, I sat down with my mother to tell her about my upcoming move to the U.S. I explained everything—the center, the care she would receive, and how they would support her. To my surprise, she was excited. She smiled at the thought of the center and said, "Don't waste your life worrying about me. You've worked so hard. Go after your dreams."

Her words stayed with me. She didn't want me to hold back because of her, and I knew she was ready for the next step. She even said she wanted to go to the center the very next day so she could settle in before I left. So, the following day, I took her there, knowing she was in good hands.

Soon after dropping her off, I received the last of my paperwork, confirming everything was set for our move. Leaving her behind was hard. Amina and I hugged her, said our goodbyes, and then walked away. Knowing we were stepping into a new chapter while she was starting her own was an emotional moment. After returning home, I called Elso to tell him about my plans. I explained everything about the immigration process, the move to the U.S., and how free we were to live the life we had always dreamed of.

I told him about my steps, the documents in place, and how I found a center for my mother. As I shared all this, I could feel the total weight of the decision setting in. Elso understood how significant this moment was. He was excited and knew this wasn't just a change of location but a natural step toward building a different life for us. We ended the conversation with understanding, both knowing this was something I had to do.

With everything in place, I focused on completing the last steps of the immigration process. After passing the medical tests, Amina and I attended our interview and were approved. It felt like a mountain had been lifted, and soon after, I bought our plane tickets. We were ready for the next chapter.

After dropping my mother at the center and saying our goodbyes, I focused on the final steps before the move. I contacted my biological father to update him on the transition to the U.S. That's when he offered to help with selling my home and belongings. I mentioned that friends would handle it, but he volunteered.

He and Brigitte came by later that day. What started as a simple conversation turned into a disagreement? My father wanted a power of attorney to sell my things, but Brigitte insisted she could manage it more quickly. After listening to them go back and forth, I signed a power of attorney to her, knowing it would move things along. Once the papers were signed, they headed out, and I had a moment to reflect on the situation.

Amina and I packed our belongings and headed to the airport after my father and Brigitte left. We checked in our luggage and boarded the plane. As we flew, my mind kept going back over everything that had brought us to this moment.

The flight attendant's voice came over the speaker, asking everyone to fasten their seatbelts. I looked over at Amina, still resting, and braced myself. We were nearing Atlanta, the place where we would begin again.

Amina pressed her face against the window as the plane touched down, her eyes wide in wonder. I could see her excitement reflecting my own, though I knew we weren't quite there yet. The wheels hit the ground, and the plane began to slow, the familiar engine hum filling the cabin. We were in Atlanta—finally.

We unbuckled our seatbelts, gathered our things, and stepped off the plane into the terminal. The airport was massive—Hartsfield-Jackson felt like a city of its own. People moved in every direction, the energy buzzing around us. Amina clung to my hand, looking around with wide eyes. 'This place is huge!' she exclaimed.

I nodded, feeling the weight of the moment settle in. But the excitement was mixed with nervousness. We still had to get through immigration, and I knew that until we passed that final checkpoint, it wasn't time to relax just yet. We followed the signs, winding through the terminal, taking in the sights around us—so many different people and languages being spoken.

As we approached the immigration line, I took a deep breath. This was the final step before we could call this place our new home.

The airport's noise surrounded us, but I could only focus on the officer ahead. Every step brought us closer. I held Amina's hand a little tighter, knowing we weren't quite there yet. Not until we crossed this threshold.

When it was our turn, I handed our documents to the immigration officer. He looked through the papers carefully. I watched his face, waiting. With a firm stamp, he handed the documents back.

"Welcome to the United States," he said.

I looked down at Amina, who grinned up at me. We had done it. This was the beginning of something new, something we had fought so hard for.

We walked through the terminal together, but before we left, I stopped, kneeling at Amina's level. "Let's thank God."

We both knelt right there in the middle of the airport and kissed the floor. I closed my eyes, thanking the Lord for guiding us through every hardship and bringing us to this moment. Amina followed her voice, which was small but filled with sincerity.

In that instant, nothing else mattered—not the challenges behind us, not the unknowns ahead—just this—a moment of gratitude and faith. We stood up, and I smiled at my daughter, knowing that after everything, we had made it. This was our new beginning. This was home.

As I reflect on my journey, I recognize the power of perseverance and hope. Despite the obstacles, I chose to rise above the challenges, not letting them define me but allowing them to shape my strength. I have learned the importance of forgiveness—not for those who hurt me, but for my peace. My grandmother's wisdom remains with me, reminding me that kindness and compassion can guide us even through the darkest times.

This chapter of my life closes with gratitude for all the lessons learned, the bonds rebuilt, and the future that lies ahead. As we settle into this new life, I believe that every step has led me here for a reason.

The journey is far from over. The next chapter will unfold with new challenges and opportunities. But for now, I find peace in knowing that this is where I was meant to be.

America is a new beginning, not just for me but for the life I am building. There's more to come, and I am ready.

About the Author

Cara Kuma Kinté was born in Douala, Cameroon, and now resides in Raleigh, North Carolina. Her life's journey has taken her across continents, from Cameroon to Belgium and the United States. These experiences have shaped her deep understanding of hope, resilience, and the strength to persevere through life's challenges.

In *The Born of Angels and Demons*, Cara shares her deeply personal story, reflecting on her struggles, triumphs, and lessons learned along the way. Inspired by her journey of overcoming adversity, she wrote this book to offer hope and strength to those facing their battles. For Cara, writing this book was not just about telling her story but about empowering others to embrace their resilience and find light in the darkest moments.

Cara's future as an author is filled with purpose. She plans to continue writing, with her next project focused on sharing more about her experiences and offering guidance to those who feel lost or voiceless. She sees storytelling as a powerful tool for healing and hopes to use her words to inspire change and foster understanding.

Beyond writing, Cara is committed to supporting causes that are close to her heart, particularly those related to homelessness, domestic violence, and individuals who feel they have no voice. She believes in giving back and hopes her book will not only uplift readers but also generate funds to support these important causes.

Cara's message to her readers is simple: *never underestimate the power of hope.* It is her wish that each person who reads her story feels encouraged to keep moving forward, no matter what the obstacles, and to believe in their ability to create a better future. Hope is unstoppable, and so are you.

Made in the USA
Columbia, SC
28 January 2025

385e6357-5bb5-46b1-acc8-f83460536c34R01